IN THE SPIRIT OF THEIR

THE THRAPSTON ROLL OF HONOUR
1914 – 2007

A TRIBUTE TO THE MEN OF THRAPSTON WHO HAVE GIVEN THEIR LIVES IN ARMED CONFLICT

COMPILED BY
ERIC FRANKLIN and EDDIE SEWELL

A THRAPSTON DISTRICT HISTORICAL SOCIETY PUBLICATION

Thrapston District Historical Society
War Memorial Research Group

is grateful to

Awards for All

for the generous grant which has made this publication possible.

First published in 2009 by

Thrapston District Historical Society
3 Fisher Close
Thrapston
Northamptonshire NN14 4UB
UK

www.thrapstonhistorysoc.co.uk

Copyright © Eric Franklin & Eddie Sewell, 2009

ISBN: 978-0-9563642-0-3

All rights reserved. No part of this publication may be reproduced in any form or by any means without permission from the authors.

Front Cover: The Peace Park Thrapston
Back Cover: Original Artwork by Mandy Dawkins

Prepared for publication by Eric Franklin & Eddie Sewell

Printed by Inkwell Printing
Units 7 – 7a, The Workshops, Barnwell,
Near Oundle, Peterborough, PE8 5PL
01832 273745
inkwellprinting@btconnect.com
www.inkwellprinting.co.uk

Contents

Acknowledgements..iv
Foreword...vi
Introduction..vii
The Authors..ix

World War 1
1914..1
1915..5
1916..19
1917..35
1918..47
1919 and 1921..69

World War 2..75

Iraq 2007...91
Stephen Edwards' Medals...94

World War 1 Rolls of Honour...97
World War 2 and Iraq Rolls of Honour..99
Other Rolls of Honour – Thrapston Baptist Church............................100
                Smith and Grace Roll of Honour............................101
                Thrapston Institute..103
                Thrapston and District Rifle Shooting Club............103

World War 1 Remembrance, War Memorials and Peace Celebrations............104

World War 1 Campaign Medals and Bronze Plaques..........................109
World War 2 Stars and Medals...111

The German White Flag Treachery..114
The Thrapston Chums..115

The Loss of HMS Glorious, June 1940..117
The Battle for Primasole Bridge, July 1943...119
Let Not Those Kind F-Words Be Lost...121
The Gallivanting Gunner From Thrapston..122

Plan of Oundle Road Cemetery Thrapston..124
Index...125

Acknowledgements

Any publication is impossible without the help of a large number of people. This one is no exception. Without the support of local organisations and individuals, including relatives of the casualties, we would not have been able to compile this tribute. The loan of papers, photographs, medals and ephemera has aided us greatly. We thank you all.

We wish to place on record our special thanks to the following.

The **Thrapston District Historical Society** for allowing us to publish under their auspices. Special mention must be made of **Neil Busby**, grant specialist and keeper of the Societies website, and **Pam Jones**, Treasurer for the Society, who administered the grant.

The **Thrapston Branch of the Royal British Legion** for their continuing encouragement, with a special mention for the late **Denis Barber** and **Philip Loaring**.

Mandy Dawkins for providing original artwork.

Our friends working on similar projects locally who never ceased in their encouragement. Special mention must be made of **Steve & Andy at Raunds** and **Ian & Geoff at Higham Ferrers**.

Joe Pigniatello and the team at **BBC Radio Northampton** for allowing us air time and for their willingness to publicise our project.

The **Evening Telegraph, Herald & Post** and **Nene Valley News** for willingness to print our press releases and advertise the project.

June Davy for putting regular updates in Jigsaw, the monthly Parish Magazine.

St. James' Church, Thrapston Baptist Church and **Thrapston Town Council** for permission to use their Rolls of Honour and the Thrapston Crest.

Staff at **Thrapston Library**.

Andrea and the staff at **Kettering Library** for patience over many months.

Caroline the Newspaper Archivist at the **Kettering Evening Telegraph**.

Staff at **Northampton and Abingdon Park Museums**.

Nigel Lutt at **Bedfordshire and Luton Archives and Records Service.**

Northampton Records Office for the use of original material.

Denis Knight and his son **Peter Knight** for permission to reproduce "Let Not Those Kind F-Words Be Lost" on page 121.

The Imperial War Museum for various photographs.

Jeanne Pike for auditing our accounts.

Michelle Goring at Forget me not, High Street, Thrapston for being our public point of sale.

Inkwell Printing for advice and patience over many months.

Our willing team of proof-readers – **Brian and Janet Hulmes**, **Liz and Raymond Bryan**, **Chris and Di Norton** and **Philip Pike**. Any errors remaining are purely the responsibility of the authors.

The following for the loan of photographs, medals and memorabilia and information –

Philip Loaring re William James Loaring
Ray Barratt re Ernest Wilfred Barratt
Ray Jeffery re Alfred Shrives Loveday
Keith Watts re Albert John Waite and Alfred Edward Waite
Nicholas Hunt re George Johnson and Frederick William Johnson
Rennie and James Stimpson re John Thomas Stimpson
David and Kath Thoday re Robert Thomas Smith
Carol Stapley and Family re Alfred Ernest Hodson
David Cullum re Aubrey Ernest Cullum
John (Jack) Bowyer re Thomas James Bowyer
Alan Edwards re Stephen James Edwards

Our long-suffering wives – **Mary Franklin and Pauline Sewell** - who have had to put up with our incessant casualty-related chatter for such a long time.

Eric Franklin & Eddie Sewell

Foreword

Welcome to "In the Springtime of their Lives". The book is dedicated to those men of Thrapston who willingly left their homes to fight to ensure that our Country could maintain its freedom but, unfortunately, did not return. As you will see there were 58 brave men who lost their lives in the 1914 – 1918 war, 44 of them have their names on the War Memorial in the church, and 14 in the 1939 – 1945 war, 11 of their names on the Memorial. These conflicts were meant to be the wars to end all wars but, as we now know it was not the case, and we are still losing far too many of our service men and women who are now fighting for the freedom of other countries. The most recent Thrapston casualty occurred in 2007.

At the time of the First World War Thrapston was a relatively small but busy market town with a population of around 1800 people and about a quarter of the men in the town went off to war, many of them joining and serving in the Northamptonshire Regiment.

It is not possible to even guess how many men and women of Thrapston went to war in 1939 – 1945, the situation was very different. People with skills in engineering, electronics and other skills not known or required in the previous conflicts, including specialist maintenance of vehicles, tanks, aircraft and ships. Quite a few volunteered and many were conscripted, but thankfully only 14 of these were lost.

Since the end of the Second World War, there have been many other conflicts and the town has sent its fair share of men to serve in them. At present, only one man has failed to return, Stephen Edwards, who died only two years ago in Iraq.

Many thanks for the creation of this book must go to Eric Franklin and Eddie Sewell for the dedication, commitment and time they have put in to make the book possible. To obtain such a comprehensive collection of photographs, mostly with their names, must have been an immense undertaking on its own.

Many thanks to you both.

Norman Byrnes

Poppy Appeal Organiser for the Thrapston Branch of the Royal British Legion

Introduction

On Sunday November 11 2007, we were in St. James' Church for the Remembrance Day Service. When the list of names was read out, we both wondered whether anyone had any information on the stories behind the names. At this time, we had not realised we had a mutual interest. We started looking into some of the names, selected at random, and found that researching names was not as difficult as we had first thought. Some six months later, during a Thrapston District Historical Society meeting, a chance comment made us realise we were actively interested in the same thing. And so the War Memorial Research Group of two started.

Originally, we hoped to produce a collection of notes which could be of use for further studies, especially by Family Historians researching Thrapston's casualties of war. As time went by, we realised that there was enough material to produce a publication of sorts.

Our starting point was the list of names carved on the oak panelling in St. James' Church. This produced 44 names from World War 1 and a further 11 from World War 2. Very quickly, we found another four names from World War 1 on the Roll of Honour, held in the same Church, who did not appear on the panels. We were also told of some names from World War 2 who were not included in either. This led us to make decisions about what criteria we would work to. After some discussion, we agreed that to be included, a casualty would have to fulfil at least one of the following –

They are named on one of the town's Rolls of Honour.
They were born in Thrapston and lived here for a number of years.
They or their parents lived in Thrapston when they died.
Their death was reported in the local press as being that of a Thrapston man.

Even with these criteria there were some names which caused a few problems. In the end, we had to make editorial decisions and decided that rather than risk omitting names erroneously, we would include them, if they had lived some of their life in town, were known to residents at the time of their death and were almost certainly not included on any other Memorial in the United Kingdom.

For much of 2008, we continued local research. This involved many hours poring over old newspapers at Kettering Library and working our way through a large number of documents. By this time we knew that there was sufficient material for a book. We had met the Raunds War Memorials Research Group and were impressed with the format they had used to commemorate their men.

The Historical Society had recently been successful in obtaining grants to set up both a Family History section and also an Oral History Project. After some discussion, it was agreed that we could make an application to Awards for All under the auspices of the Historical Society. A number of months work finally had our grant bid prepared and, after a couple of hiccups, we were awarded the full amount we had estimated it would cost to produce a quality publication. The grant was time-limited, so we knew we had twelve months to come up with the final product.

The title "In the Springtime of their Lives" is taken from the Illuminated Roll of Honour in St. James' Church.
    "We mourn – though Pride is mingled with our tears – our best and bravest, some had made a name on other fields, and some were new to fame, but none had passed the Springtime of their lives."

All the biographies have been compiled chronologically by date of death. From the onset, we had hoped to include photographs of the men. Most have been obtained from the Kettering Leader (World War 1) and the Thrapston Raunds and Oundle Journal (World War 2). We are especially grateful to relatives and other sources who have lent us original photographs. Mandy Dawkin's sketch of a Tommy has been used where no picture has been found for World War 1 casualties. Some casualties appear on Memorials elsewhere and where possible, we have included this information. We trust that you find it easy to follow. Eddie has produced a comprehensive index to aid finding specific names and places.

Following the biographies, we list all casualties mentioned in this book and basic details and sources. We have included details about the other Rolls of Honour we discovered existed, but have been unable to find.

A number of articles follow, including **"The White Flag Treachery"**, **Campaign Medals Issued**, some history of the **Rolls of Honour, World War 1 Peace Celebrations and the Memorials** and **"The Battle for Primasole Bridge"**, all of which, we hope, will enhance this tribute.

The memory of the 73 men whose stories we have included still lives. Their deeds will never be forgotten. Heroes all, we dedicate this book to them.

May they continue to rest in Peace

Eric Franklin & Eddie Sewell
November 2009

The Authors

Eric Franklin

Born in Mitcham, Surrey in 1949. Moved to Northamptonshire in 1973 and Thrapston in 1982. Worked for Social Services in Northamptonshire and Cambridgeshire for over 25 years. Now retired. A member of the History Society for a number of years and the current Editor of Strapetona, the Society's annual magazine. A Thrapston Town Councillor, he was Mayor 2006 – 2007. Married to Mary with three children now all living away.
This is his first publication.

Eddie Sewell

Born in Braunschweig, Germany in 1946. Lived in NW London from 1948. Joined the Metropolitan Police in 1970 serving in outer and central London. Retired in 2000 and moved to Thrapston. Currently a Town Councillor and Chairman of Thrapston Heritage Centre Trust. Also Programme Secretary of the Historical Society. Married to Pauline for 42 years, their married son and daughter have also moved to Thrapston, with grandsons attending local schools. Enjoys bowls with Islip Bowls Club.

Every attempt has been made to establish copyright holders of pictures we have used in this book. The following are specifically acknowledged –

St James' Church page 106
Thrapston Baptist Church page 100
Thrapston Town Council pages 102, 138
Bedfordshire and Luton Archives and Records Service page 38
(Bedfordshire and Luton Archives and Records Service (X550/1/81) – Gerald Lenton
Northampton Records Office pages 3 and 105
(Northamptonshire Record Office (325p/271/1) – Philip Makin
(Northamptonshire Record Office (325p/138) – Drawing and Invitation
The Imperial War Museum pages 120 and 123
Philip Loaring pages 38 and 110
Ray Barratt page 72
Keith Watts page 110
Nicholas Hunt pages 49 and 73
Rennie and James Stimpson page 58
Carol Stapley and Family page 82
David Cullum page 83
John (Jack) Bowyer page 81
Eddie Sewell page 89 and sketches page 118
Eric Franklin front cover, pages 108, 114 and sketch page 124

We apologise for any inadvertent omissions and will, of course, willingly amend and acknowledge such in any future edition.

EF & ES
2009

1914

Philip Makin..November 3 1914
Walter Miller..November 3 1914

Philip Makin
May 1894 – November 3 1914

Private Philip Makin was born in Nottingham during May 1894, the eldest child of Philip and Lavinia Makin. By 1901, his family had moved to Thrapston and lived in Oundle Road, Mr. Makin working as an ironfounder. By the onset of War, the family lived in Halford Street. Philip was a member of Thrapston Church Choir and frequently sang at entertainments in the town and neighbourhood. He specialised in humorous songs.

He enlisted with the 1st Battalion, Northamptonshire Regiment, Service Number 9698, in Northampton, 18 months before the outbreak of War. He was one of the eight members of the Northamptonshire Regiment who survived a treacherous onslaught by German troops under a white flag. See page 114 for fuller details.

He was wounded in the neck at Ypres, Belgium on November 2 1914 and died in hospital of his wounds the next day. The Regimental War Diary for the period October 26 to November 15 has been lost, although they were heavily engaged for most of this time. Between October 25 and November 5, the Regiment suffered 1680 casualties, Philip being one of them. He is buried at the Ypres Town Cemetery Extension, Plot II. B. 19. He was awarded the 1914 Star and Clasp, and the British War and Victory Medals.

A joint Memorial Service was held in Thrapston Parish Church on Wednesday December 9 1914 for Philip and Private Walter Miller (page 4), who died on the same day. A detachment of the 1st Thrapston Troop of Baden-Powell's Scouts attended the service in full uniform.

Walter Miller
1883 – November 3 1914

Private Walter Miller was born in Thrapston in 1883, the third eldest son. By 1891, his mother, Martha, was widowed and the family lived in Titchmarsh Lane (now Oundle Road). By the 1901 Census, his mother had re-married to Marshall Meadows. The family still lived in Oundle Road. Walter was a general labourer.

Walter joined the Army circa 1904, enlisting in Northampton and served in India for nearly seven years. He remained in the Reserve after leaving the Army for two years, before rejoining the colours on the outbreak of War. During these two years, he worked at the Islip Furnaces and married only a year before the War started. He was a member of the Northamptonshire Regiment, 1st Battalion, Service Number 7621. He was one of the eight members of the Northamptonshire Regiment who survived a treacherous onslaught by German troops under a white flag. See page 114 for further details.

He was wounded and admitted to hospital on about November 2 1914. He died the next day of his wounds and was interred in the Poperinghe Old Military Cemetery Belgium, Grave I. L. 50. He was awarded the 1914 Star and Clasp and the British War and Victory Medals.

He is commemorated on his mother's (Martha Meadows) headstone at Oundle Road Cemetery, Thrapston, Grave Number 182, along with his brother Herbert, (page 33) who appears later in this book.

A joint Memorial Service was held in Thrapston Parish Church on Wednesday December 9 1914 for him and Private Philip Makin (page 3), who died on the same day. A detachment of the 1st Thrapston Troop of Baden-Powell's Scouts attended the service in full uniform.

1915

Basil Frederick Emery..February 17 1915
Alfred Edward Waite..March 14 1915
William Edward Cooper...March 26 1915
William Reeve..March 26 1915
Herbert Frederick Gilbert..April 21 1915
George Samuel Earle..May 9 1915
John Thomas Giddings...May 9 1915
Richard Edis Templeman..May 9 1915
Albert John Waite...September 25 1915
Charles Edward Richardson..October 5 1915
George Henry Simpson...October 13 1915

Basil Frederick Emery
March 23 1892 – February 17 1915

Warrant Telegraphist Basil Frederick Emery was born in Thrapston on March 23 1892, the only child of Frederick and Elizabeth Emery. His parents were schoolteachers at Thrapston School, Mr. Emery being headteacher. Basil was educated at the Thrapston School, then at Laxton Grammar School, Oundle, and became an accomplished pianist.

On leaving school, he became a learner at Thrapston Post Office aged 15 years. After about three years general experience, he qualified for the wireless branch of the Post Office and was stationed at Niton, St. Catherine's Point, Isle of Wight. At this time, he was the youngest Wireless Officer in the Post Office. He stayed at Niton for nearly two years, before transferring to Brow Head, Ireland where he worked for three months.

He resigned and joined the Marconi International Marine Communications Co. Ltd. as a Wireless Telegraphist. He joined the SS Canada (Dominion Line) and made two crossings of the Atlantic from Liverpool to Montreal, Canada. He transferred to the Oriana (Pacific Steam Navigation Company) and made one trip between Liverpool and the west coast of South America. He joined the White Star Line and, leaving Liverpool, sailed on the Delphie around the world, returning to London at the end of March 1913. He had one day's leave, making a flying visit to Thrapston, before signing up for a three year term on the Royal Mail steamer Arankola, sailing between Calcutta and Rangoon. On the outbreak of war the vessel was requisitioned by military authorities, and was used to transport Indian troops to Marseilles and other ports. On January 31 1915, he was admitted to Bombay Hospital with appendicitis and died on February 17 1915, probably being buried locally. His name was recorded in the Roll of Honour and carved on the panels in St. James' Church. Basil's name does not appear on the Commonwealth War Graves Commission site. As far as is known, he was not awarded any medals.

(There is no known photograph of Basil – he is probably in the above picture taken in 1900).

Alfred Edward Waite
1897 – March 14 1915

Private Alfred Edward Waite was born in Guider Street, Cambridge in 1897, the sixth child of Albert and Mary Waite and younger brother of Albert John Waite (page 15), who also died during the War. By 1901, they lived in Thrapston, in a Yard off Victoria Terrace, Mr. Waite being a fishmonger. After leaving school, he worked for Alfred Hensman, a Thrapston builder.

He enlisted with the Northamptonshire Regiment, 2nd Battalion, Service Number 12808 in Northampton on August 31 1914 and went to the front on February 23 1915.

He was killed in action at Neuve Chapelle, France on March 14 1915. The Battalion War Diary for that day states that they were in their billets at Rouge Croix until 6.00pm, which were heavily shelled. Initially, Alfred was reported as being "missing". The family received official confirmation of his death from the War Office on August 20 1915.

He is commemorated on the Le Touret Memorial, France, on Panel 29. He has no known grave. He was awarded the 1914/15 Star and British War and Victory medals.

A Memorial Service was held at Thrapston Parish Church for him and Private Herbert Frederick Gilbert (page 11) on Sunday August 29 1915.

William Edward Cooper
1892 – March 26 1915

Private William Edward Cooper was born in Thrapston in 1892, the second oldest child of Edward and Annie Cooper. In 1901, the family were living in Halford Street. On leaving school, he worked at the Ironstone Pits at Twywell. He wrote home very bright and interesting letters, including references to trench life, and some of these were read at meetings of the Thrapston Men's Adult School, of which he was a member and where he attended regularly.

He enlisted with the 1st Battalion Northamptonshire Regiment a few days after the outbreak of war, Service Number 12915, and sailed for the Front on February 1 1915. He celebrated his 23rd Birthday at the Front. He was a tall man, this being the cause of his receiving the fatal wound to his head, which was a little above the trench, in the La Quinque Rue, Chocat Menier Corner Sector on March 26 1915.

He was buried by his comrades, who held him in high esteem, at the Guards Cemetery, Windy Corner, Cuinchy, France, Grave Number IV. J. 4. He was awarded the 1914/1915 Star and British War and Victory medals.

A Memorial Service was held for him and Private William Reeve (page 10), who died on the same day, at Thrapston Parish Church on Sunday April 18 1915, attended by Thrapston Town Band, the Fire Brigade and the Boy Scouts.

William Reeve
July 15 1897 – March 26 1915

Private William Reeve was born in Towcester, Northamptonshire, the oldest child of Thomas and Rose Reeve. By 1901, the family had moved to Pleasant Row, Islip, where his father worked as a general labourer. Mr. Reeve died in circa 1912 and by the outbreak of War, Mrs. Reeve had moved to Oundle Road.

William enlisted with the Northamptonshire Regiment, Service Number 12970, on August 30 1914 in Northampton, being in the 2nd Battalion. He went to the Front on February 24 1915.

He was wounded by a gunshot to his head at Neuve Chapelle on March 14 1915 alongside Alfred Waite who was killed outright. His initial wound was bandaged by George Earle (page 12) who then helped carry him to the Dressing Station. He was admitted to the 11th General Hospital, British Expeditionary Force, Boulogne on the same day, but died of his wounds twelve days later on March 26 1915. He is buried in the Boulogne Eastern Cemetery in Grave Number III. D. 63. He was awarded the 1914/1915 Star and British War and Victory medals.

A Memorial Service was held for him and Private William Edward Cooper (page 9), who died on the same day, at Thrapston Parish Church on Sunday April 18 1915, attended by Thrapston Town Band, the Fire Brigade and the Boy Scouts.

Herbert Frederick Gilbert
1894 – April 21 1915

Private Herbert Frederick Gilbert was born in 1894 at Croxton, Cambridgeshire, the second oldest child of James and Emma Gilbert. In 1901, they lived at The Slatiles, Croxton, Mr. Gilbert being employed as a coachman.

Herbert enlisted with the 2nd Battalion Bedfordshire Regiment, Service Number 14634 in Bedford in September 1914, later transferring to the 1st Battalion. He went to the front on March 24 1915.

He was killed in action on April 21 1915 at Reningelst during heavy enemy bombardment, one of over 400 casualties that day, and is commemorated on the Menin Gate Memorial, Ypres, Panel 31 and 33. He has no known grave, although there were reports that he had been buried by the Germans at Hill 60, near Ypres. His death was not confirmed until August 1915. He was awarded the 1914/1915 Star, British War and Victory medals.

At the time of his death, his parents were living in Thrapston at "Neneside", Midland Road.

A Memorial Service was held at the Parish Church for him and Private Alfred Edward Waite (page 8) on Sunday August 29 1915.

George Samuel Earle
1882 – May 9 1915

Lance Corporal George Samuel Earle was born in Walsall, Staffordshire in 1882. By 1890 they were living in Titchmarsh, later moving to Denford Lodge near Thrapston.

A career soldier, in 1901, he enlisted in Portland, Dorset as a Private with the 2nd Northamptonshire Regiment, Service Number 6231, based at the Verne Citadel, Portland, Dorset. He married Rachel Smith of Aldwincle in 1913, their home being at 10 Hill Street, Kettering.

At the time of his death aged 33, on May 9 1915, he was serving with the 1st Battalion, Northamptonshire Regiment. He died at Aubers Ridge on the same day as Richard Templeman.

He is remembered on the Le Touret Memorial, France, on Panel 29 with two Thrapston comrades and has no known grave. He was awarded the 1914 Star and Clasp, British War and Victory medals.

A combined Memorial Service was held to commemorate him and Privates Richard Templeman (page 14) and Albert "Jack" Waite (page 15), on October 10 1915 at St James' Church. He is not included on any of the Thrapston Rolls of Honour.

John Thomas Giddings
1889 – May 9 1915

Private John Thomas Giddings was born in 1889 in Streaton, Illinois, U.S.A., the second child and only son of John Henry and Mary Ann Giddings. John was a labourer who originally came from Oundle. The family left the U.S.A. in 1891 and arrived in Liverpool on September 1 on the "Lord Gough". By 1901, the family were living in Halford Street, Mr. Giddings being employed in the Ironstone Quarries. On leaving school, John worked at Smith and Grace's Iron Foundry. A keen footballer, he was one of the founding members of Thrapston United Football Club, played wing back and was Vice Captain for a couple of years. He was also a member of the Church Choir.

He enlisted in Northampton with the 8th Battalion of the Northamptonshire Regiment, Service Number 13828, shortly after the War began, transferred to the 2nd Battalion and sailed to France on March 25 1915, after a period of training at Weymouth.

He had not been at the Front for many weeks when he was killed in action on May 9 1915 at Sailly near Armentieres. The Battalion were ordered to advance at 5.50am and were instantly faced with heavy machine gun fire. Tommy was but one of many killed that day. Jack Waite (page 15) wrote to his wife after the battle "we had a bit of a rough time last Sunday. Poor Bill Mehew got wounded in the hand, and was trying to get back and was killed: and Tommy Giddings was killed: and those who were left got back the best that they could… I am alright, and I don't want to go through another lot like it. I was a bit lucky".

He is remembered on the Ploegsteert Memorial, Belgium on Panel 7. He has no known grave. He was awarded the 1914/1915 Star, British War and Victory medals.

A Memorial Service was held for him at Thrapston Parish Church on Sunday July 25 1915.

Richard Edis Templeman
1892 – May 9 1915

Private Richard Edis Templeman was born in Thrapston, the youngest of five children born to Edis Alfred and Mary Ann Templeman. He had two brothers, Alfred and Fred and two sisters, Etta and Bertha (who died young). His father was a foundry labourer and then a groom. The family lived in Huntingdon Road in 1901. In about 1910, he was a member of Thrapston Argyll Football Club as were John Giddings and John Pollard.

He enlisted with the Northamptonshire Regiment in Northampton at the outbreak of War, Service Number 12930, being in the 1st. Battalion. He was killed in action at Aubers Ridge, struck by shrapnel whilst advancing on May 9 1915, aged 23, although official confirmation was not received by his family until October 1915. Of 750 men in the Battalion who started the day, only 150 remained unscathed. One of his comrades wrote to Mrs. Templeman "Having seen your son's photo in the paper, and being one of his chums, I consider it my duty to write and let you know that Dick was killed while running forward at St. Aubers Ridge on May 9th. He was struck by a piece of shell and killed outright. I saw him fall, but had to go on, and never saw any more of him. Your son was a brave lad, and was well liked by all who knew him, and we who have got through wounded are very sorry he is not with us now, but he died a brave soldier's death, as many more of my chums died that fateful morning".

He is commemorated on the Le Touret Memorial, France on Panel 29. He has no known grave. He was awarded the 1914/1915 Star and British War and Victory medals.

A Memorial Service was held at the Parish Church on Sunday October 10 1915 for him, Lance-Corpl. George Earle (page 12) and Private Jack Waite (page 15), the pulpit being dressed with the Union Jack.

Albert John Waite
1887 – September 25 1915

Private Albert John Waite, known as Jack, was born in Marlborough, Wiltshire in 1887, the oldest child of Albert and Mary Waite, and elder brother of Alfred Edward Waite (page 8) who also died during the War. By 1901 the family lived in the Yard off Victoria Terrace, Thrapston, Mr. Waite being a fishmonger. By 1911 he had married Mabel and lived at New Town, Woodford. Jack worked as a furnace labourer. He was a member of Thrapston Town Harriers and had much success. On one occasion, he was the Midlands Cross-Country Champion.

Albert enlisted in Kettering with the 2nd Battalion, Northamptonshire Regiment, Service Number 16506, in November 1914, one of four brothers to enlist, three in the Northamptonshire Regiment.

He went to France on April 15 1915 and was killed in action on September 25 1915 at Bois Grenier when a shell landed in the trench he and a comrade were occupying. He left a widow and three children.

He is remembered on the Ploegsteert Memorial, Belgium on Panel 7. He has no known grave. He was awarded the 1914/1915 Star and the British War and Victory medals.

A Memorial Service was held at the Parish Church on October 10 1915 for him, Lance-Corpl. George Earle (page 12) and Private Richard Edis Templeman (page 14).

Charles Edward Richardson
1893 – October 5 1915

Private Charles Edward Richardson was born in about 1893, probably in Spalding, Lincolnshire. He was the only child of Edward and Mrs. Richardson. In 1901, it is possible that they lived in Islip. By 1905, the family were in Wadenhoe. Charles started working for Mr. Whitney of Pilton the next year, and maintained this employment until he joined the Army. Latterly, he worked as an engine driver, probably a traction engine, on a farm. The family moved to Aldwincle in about 1912 and finally to Oundle Road, Thrapston at the beginning of 1915.

Charles joined the Northamptonshire Regiment, 1/4th Battalion, at Northampton on April 5 1915, Service Number 3964. He went to the Dardanelles, Turkey on July 28 1915 and was killed in action at Hill 60 on October 5 1915. There is no record in the Battalion War Diary for this date.

He was buried initially at 1/4th Northants Cemetery and re-interred at 7 Field Ambulance Cemetery, Gallipoli, Turkey after the Armistice, Grave Number II. D. 9. He was awarded the 1914/1915 Star, British War and Victory medals.

George Henry Simpson
1896 – October 13 1915

Private George Henry Simpson was born in Glinton, Northamptonshire (now Cambridgeshire) in 1896, the youngest of George H. and Jane Simpson's five children. In 1901, they lived in Foundry Yard, Glinton, where Mr. Simpson was a blacksmith. By September 1914, the family were living in Thurning. By October 1915, Mr. Simpson and one of his daughters lived in Oundle Road, Thrapston, Mrs. Simpson having died.

It was from Thurning that George enlisted in Peterborough, joining the Northamptonshire Regiment, 5th Battalion, Service Number 15990, even though he was later reported in the local press as "not a very strong youth".

George went to France on May 31 1915. He was wounded in the leg and head early on October 13 1915, losing much blood, in the trenches north of Vermelles, near Bethune. Within half an hour, he was bandaged at a Dressing Station, but died later that day, one of five men lost by the Battalion during the day's action. In the whole of 1915, only 41 men of the 5th Battalion were killed. George wrote home regularly, the last letter from him arriving the day before the official notification of his death.

He is buried at Bethune Town Cemetery, France, Grave Number IV. E. 16.
He was awarded the 1914/1915 Star and British War and Victory medals.

1916

George Abery Unger...January 7 1916
Alexander John Emery..March 7 1916
Arthur Edward Warren..June 1 1916
John Isaac Ashton Sutcliffe..June 5 1916
John Robert Pollard..July 7 1916
John Samuel Smith...July 29 1916
Horace Dingley...August 8 1916
George Ernest Nicholls..August 10 1916
George Edward Arnold..August 24 1916
Percy John Holley..August 27 1916
Hugh David Hall...September 10 1916
George William Turner...October 9 1916
Herbert Miller...October 23 1916
George Alfred Langley...October 25 1916

George Abery Unger
1889 – January 7 1916

Bombardier George Abery Unger was born at Holborn Workhouse, City Road, Shoreditch, London on December 24 1889, the day his mother was admitted from Kings Cross Police Station. His mother was Louisa Unger, born in Wartenburg, Germany in about 1871, formerly a nursery governess. No father is named on his Birth Certificate. In 1891, Louisa was staying at the House of Mercy, Ditchingham, Norfolk. It appears she was married in 1897, possibly to a Mr. Johnson. By 1891, George was living with Mrs. Mary Stanion at The Green, Islip, probably boarded out by the Holborn Board of Governors. Also at the address in Islip was Louisa Riches, aged 8 years, also a boarder who kept in touch with him in later life. George was brought up by Mrs. Stanion until, it is believed, 1899, when she died. George then moved into the Thrapston Union, where he is recorded on the 1901 census, and attended Thrapston Church School under the care of Mr. Emery. Currently, his circumstances are under investigation, but at some time, he moved to live with Mrs. Holley in Market Road and would have known her son Percy, who was also a casualty of the war (page 30).

George had enlisted with the Royal Field Artillery, Service Number 50406 in London by 1911 and was attached to "B" Battery, 98th Brigade. He went to France on September 4 1915, moving to Salonika shortly after, and within four months, was killed by a direct hit from a shell. He was buried by his comrades, the burial also being attended by the General Commanding Divisional Artillery, and after the war, re-interred in Grave Number 1376, Mikra British Cemetery, Greece. He was awarded the 1914/1915 Star, British and Victory medals.

George is not mentioned in any of the Thrapston Rolls of Honour. His death was reported to Mr. Emery, Headmaster of Thrapston Church School by Louisa Riches, by then living in London. His death was reported in the Northamptonshire Evening Telegraph on Monday February 21 1916 and headed "Former Thrapston Schoolboy Killed".

Alexander John Emery
1889 - March 7 1916

Private Alexander John Emery was born in Woburn, Bedfordshire, in 1889, the fourth of eight children born to William and Emily Emery. William was a master grocer. He started work for Mr. A. H. Touch, outfitter, in Thrapston at about the beginning of 1914 and, although only a resident of the town for a year or so, immersed himself in the community. He attended the Baptist Church, was actively involved with the Christian Endeavour and taught in the Sunday School. He was also on the committee of the Thrapston Shop Assistants Social Club. He moved to Northampton at the beginning of 1915, working for Messrs. Adnitt Brothers.

He married Ada Robinson in Northampton during the summer of 1915, setting up home at 9 Fife Street, Northampton, just after enlisting with the 7th Battalion of the Northamptonshire Regiment, Service Number 18450. After a period of training, he went to France in September 1915 and then to the front on October 5 1915.

He was killed on March 7 1916, shot through the heart whilst erecting barbed wire and gas curtains in the snow at Zillebeke Lake with a party of Royal Engineers. A comrade wrote "There is not one of his chums but has the memory of some kindness performed by him. Nothing was too much trouble for him, especially on behalf of those who were not well".

He is buried at the Menin Road South Military Cemetery, Grave Number I. I. 12. He was awarded the 1914/1915 Star, British and Victory Medals.

He is not mentioned on any Thrapston Roll of Honour. His death was recorded in both the Evening Telegraph and Kettering Guardian in the "Thrapston" section and he was considered to be a Thrapston man at the time.

Arthur Edward Warren
1895 - June 1 1916

Private Arthur Edward Warren was born in 1895 on Jersey. For the first twelve or thirteen years he was raised by his grandmother in Denford. On her death, he went to live with an aunt, Mrs. Warren at South Terrace, Market Road, Thrapston. He worked for a short time for Mr. Essex in Denford, before moving to Messrs. Freeman and Webb of Thrapston as a builders labourer. He was for some years a member of the Denford Church Choir and Sunday School.

He enlisted on September 8 1913 as an underage boy with the Royal Marine Light Infantry, Service Number PO/16891. He joined Leviathan on November 8 1914, having previously been at the Depots in Deal, Kent and Portsmouth, before transferring to HMS Tipperary on June 2 1915. He was serving on the Tipperary at the Battle of Jutland, which occurred between May 31 and June 1 1916. The ship left Scapa Flow late on May 30. At 12.03am on June 1, the German Dreadnought, SMS Westfalen opened fire on Tipperary with her secondary 5.9inch (15cm) armament. Tipperary was raked with 92 rounds of 5.9inch and 45 rounds of 3.5 inch shells, which reduced her to a blazing wreck within minutes, carrying away her bridge and all on it. At 1.10am the German torpedo boats S53 and G88 encountered the burning wreck of the Tipperary and rescued 8 crew members from a raft in its proximity. At approximately 2.00am on June 1 1916, HMS Tipperary finally sank. 185 men died on the ship, including Arthur Warren, and only twelve survived, eight of whom were taken prisoner of war. His body was recovered on June 25 1916 and identified through his identity disc and letters and papers in his pockets.

He is buried at Kviberg Cemetery, Sweden, Grave Number 2. C. 9. He was awarded the 1914/1915 Star and British War and Victory medals.

He is not mentioned on any of the Thrapston Rolls of Honour but is named on the Denford War Memorial.

John Isaac Ashton Sutcliffe
August 17 1890 – June 5 1916

Private John Isaac Ashton Sutcliffe was born in Thrapston on August 17 1890, the second son of John and Nelly Sutcliffe. In 1891, the family lived in Fair Lane (now Chancery Lane), Mr. Sutcliffe being a corn merchant. They were at the same address in 1901, Mr. Sutcliffe adding farmer to his corn merchant business. John emigrated to Canada in 1909 and by 1911, the Canadian Census shows that he was living in Township 30 in ranges 22 in the Humboldt District of Saskatchewan, about 150 miles north of Regina and working as a carpenter. By 1914 his parents had moved to Billinghay, Lincoln.

He enlisted with the 1st Canadian Mounted Rifles (Saskatchewan Regiment), Service Number 108565, on December 30 1914. He sailed for England on June 12 1915, going to France on September 22 1915. John was killed on June 5 1916. His younger brother, Corporal Harold Sutcliffe, who also went to Canada, was at the London Headquarters of the Canadian Force and was engaged in verifying official lists, when he came across the name of his brother amongst the men reported as "missing" towards the end of the month.

He is commemorated on the Menin Gate Memorial, Belgium, Panels 30 and 32. He has no known grave. We have not been able to find the appropriate medal rolls although it is likely that he was awarded the 1914/1915 Star and the British War and Victory medals.

John is also commemorated in the Canadian First World War Book of Remembrance, page 170.

John Robert Pollard
1890 – July 7 1916

Private John Robert Pollard was born in Thrapston in 1890, the second son of John T. and Clara Pollard. In 1891, they lived in Halford Street, Mr. Pollard working as a carpenter. In 1901, they were still in Halford Street and Mr. Pollard was working as an engineers pattern maker. John was a member of Thrapston Argyll Football Club alongside John Giddings and Richard Templeman, playing in goal. The picture of him was extracted from a team photograph taken in 1910. On leaving school, John became an apprentice moulder at Smith and Grace's Foundry, with whom he remained until the outbreak of war.

He enlisted in Northampton on September 2 1914 with the 2nd Battalion, Northamptonshire Regiment, Service Number 13827. He sailed to France in June 1915. Prior to his death, he was slightly wounded once by shrapnel. He was killed in action on July 7 1916 during the Battle of the Somme at Fricourt Contalmaison when the Battalion advanced into heavy machine gun fire whilst also being shelled by enemy artillery.

He is commemorated on the Thiepval Memorial, France on the Pier and Face 11D. He has no known grave. He was awarded the 1914/1915 Star and the British War and Victory medals.

John Samuel Smith
1884 – July 29 1916

Private John Samuel Smith (known as Jack) was born in Thrapston in 1884, the second son of Jeremiah and Louisa Smith. In the 1891 census, they are recorded as living in Halford Street, Mr. Smith working as a furnace labourer at Smith and Grace Iron Founders. Mrs. Smith died during the middle part of 1891 and Mr. Smith remarried in 1892 to Mary Elizabeth Dodson. In 1901, the family still lived in Halford Street. By this time, John was an apprentice bricklayer.

By about 1904, John had joined the 1st Battalion Northamptonshire Regiment, Service Number 7686, and was to see five years service in India. A reservist, he enlisted in Thrapston and rejoined his Regiment on the outbreak of war, having been working as a Platelayer for the Midland Railway, based at Kettering.

He married Florence M. Franks (born 1893 in Biggleswade, Hertfordshire) in Kettering in 1914, their daughter Catherine being born the following year.

He was shot in the jaw at Contalmaison during an attack on Munster Alley on July 22 1916 and died seven days later at the Queen Alexandra Military Extension Hospital, London aged 32. His body was transported to Thrapston by train on July 31 1916, the funeral, with full military honours, taking place the next day at the Parish Church.

He was buried at Oundle Road Cemetery in Plot C 149, the customary three shot volley being fired over his grave. His name is recorded in the Oundle Road Cemetery Burial Book, entry Number 320. Details of the funeral were given extensive coverage in local papers. After the War, a headstone was erected by the Commonwealth War Graves Commission at Thrapston Cemetery. John is named on the Thrapston and Kettering Rolls of Honour, and his name is inscribed on the Kettering War Memorial. He was awarded the 1914 Star and Clasp, British War and Victory medals.

Horace Dingley
1891 to August 8 1916

Private Horace Dingley was born in 1891, the seventh of eight sons of Albert and Susannah Dingley. Initially living at 5 South Terrace, they had moved to Midland Road by 1901. He attended Thrapston Council School and appears in a school photograph dated 1900. His father and brothers worked in the iron industry. For the two years before he enlisted, he worked in the engine room at Northampton Hospital.

He was attested in Northampton on September 7 1914, when he was lodging in Northampton at 43, Melbourne Road. He initially joined the East Surrey Regiment, Service Number 3066 and went to France in April 1915, but was transferred to the Machine Gun Corps, Service Number 49714 in December of that year. At the beginning of April 1916, he was in Egypt and on May 18 1916, he went to Salonika, Greece.

He acted as an officer's servant in Greece, where he contracted malignant malaria, dying on August 8 1916. Six days before his death he wrote to one of his brothers "I have been feeling very queer this last few days. I went sick this morning, and the doctor gave me some pills so I think I shall be alright in a day or two." His officer later wrote to his family paying tribute to Horace.

He was buried at a little cemetery for British soldiers at the village of Paprat, next to a soldier of the Buffs who died from the same cause. He was later moved to Lahana Military Cemetery, Greece, Plot II, Grave E. 1. He was awarded the 1914/1915 Star, British and Victory medals.

George Ernest Nicholls
1894 – August 10 1916

Private George Nicholls was born in Thrapston in 1894, the second youngest of nine children born to Thomas and Ann Nicholls. In 1901, the family lived in Church Lane, Mr. Nicholls being a whitestone labourer. In about 1910, George was part of a group of friends, whose picture was reproduced in The Kettering Leader in 1916 entitled Sporting Thrapston Boys. By the time of his death, the family lived in Chancery Lane.

George enlisted in the Northamptonshire Regiment, 5th Battalion, Service Number 18851, in Thrapston. He went to France on November 30 1915 and was killed in action on August 10 1916 at Aveluy France whilst on a trench digging party with the rest of "C" Company.

He is buried at Pozieres British Cemetery, Ovillers-La Boiselle, France, Grave Number I. C. 46. He was awarded the 1914/1915 Star, British War and Victory medals.

George Edward Arnold
1895 - August 24 1916

Private George Edward Arnold was born in Denford in 1895, the second oldest child of Henry and Jane Elizabeth Arnold. In 1901, they lived in High Street, Denford, Mr. Arnold being employed as a labourer in a Stone Quarry. Before the War, George frequently assisted the bell ringers in Denford. For five years he worked for Mr. T. Freeman, farmer, of Denford, who frequently sent him parcels. For some time before he joined up he was employed at Islip Furnaces.

George enlisted in the 5th Battalion Northamptonshire Regiment, Service Number 18165, in Northampton on April 21 1915 and went to France at the end of August 1915. He was shot in the right femur at Berneville, France on August 14 and by August 16 he was at the No. 1 Canadian General Hospital, Etaples. After initially making progress, gangrene set in and he died in hospital on August 24 1916. He was buried at Etaples Military Cemetery, France, Grave IX. F. 17A. He was awarded the 1914/1915 Star, British War and Victory medals.

At the time of his death, his parents lived in Market Road, Thrapston.

He is not commemorated on the Memorial in St. James' Church although his name is recorded in the Roll of Honour in the Church, but with the initial J. His name is also recorded on the Denford War Memorial.

Percy John Holley
1895 – August 27 1916

Private Percy John Holley was born in 1895 in St. Neots, Huntingdonshire, the second son of James and Sarah Jane Holley. By 1901, the family had moved to Thrapston and lived in Market Road, Mr. Holley being employed as a postal messenger.

Percy initially enlisted with the Huntingdon Cyclists Battalion, Service Number 1508 in Huntingdon on September 11 1915. He was transferred to 1/1 Battalion, Hertfordshire Regiment, Service Number 20829 on July 29 1916 before being compulsorily transferred to the $1/8^{th}$ Battalion, Royal Warwickshire Regiment, Service Number 307703 on August 6 1916. On August 27 1916, the Battalion carried out an assault on enemy trenches near Aveluy, which was the last time his comrades saw him. He was listed as "Missing on August 27 1916" on August 29 1916. A year later, he was presumed killed, the date given as August 27 1916. In November 1916, his mother received a letter from one of Percy's comrades, Private Miles, who was with him before the battalion went into a charge, but lost him afterwards. He said of Percy "He was a splendid soldier; I was taken ill while we were marching up the line, and he carried my rifle and pack for miles for me, and has looked after me night and day until I was better. He always kept cheerful and never grumbled".

The Thrapston Roll of Honour in the Parish Church lists him as "Missing" and he is not included on the carved list. He is commemorated on the Thiepval Memorial, France on the Pier and Face 9B and has no known grave. He was awarded the British War and Victory medals.

On Sunday December 26 1926, at the close of the evening service, Mr. and Mrs. Holley presented Thrapston Baptist Church with an oak reading desk, with engraved plaque, as a memorial to Percy. Sadly, its current whereabouts is unknown.

Hugh David Hall
1895 – September 10 1916

Private Hugh David Hall, usually known as David, and referred to as such in this biography, was born in 1895 at Earl's Croom, near Upton Upon Severn, Worcestershire, the third child of John Daniel and Mary Hall. In 1901, the family were living in Marston St. Lawrence near Brackley, Northamptonshire where his father worked as a domestic groom and gardener. By 1909, the family were living in Thrapston. His younger brother, Robert, is recorded as being admitted to Thrapston Council School in that year.

David was working at Beeston, near Nottingham in 1914, and enlisted in Nottingham on August 6 1914 with the Grenadier Guards, Service Number 17157, in the 3rd Battalion, and corresponded regularly with his family, many letters being reported in local newspapers. By November 16 1914 he was at the front lines, a letter in the Northamptonshire Evening Telegraph being printed on November 19. He subsequently transferred to the 1st Battalion. His brothers, John and Robert also served during the War, John with the Army Service Corps and Robert with the Northamptonshire Regiment. Both his brothers survived and are recorded in the Thrapston Roll of Honour in St. James Church. By 1916, the family home was in Horton's Lane.

He survived the bloody battle at Neuve Chapelle in 1915, where a number of his friends from Thrapston lost their lives. David was killed in action on September 10 1916 during the Battle of the Somme, just five days before the tank made its first appearance on the field of battle.

He is commemorated on the Thiepval Memorial, France on the Pier and Face 8D. He has no known grave. He was awarded the 1914 Star and Clasp, British War and Victory medals.

A Memorial Service was held for him in Thrapston on Sunday October 1 1916.

George William Turner
1897 – October 9 1916

Gunner George William Turner was born in Thrapston in 1897, the third son of George and Ada Turner. In 1901, the family lived in Halford Street, Mr. Turner being employed as an ostler's groom. For some time, he was a member of the Thrapston Church Choir. Before joining the Army George was employed at Mr. Hyde's boot factory at Rushden.

George enlisted in the Royal Sussex Regiment in Kettering, Service Number 11769 in May 1916, transferring later to the Machine Gun Corps, Service Number 46315. He went to France on September 24 1916.

He was killed in action on October 9 1916. His commanding officer wrote to his mother on October 13 - "I am sorry to inform you that your son was reported "missing" on the night of October 9th. He was guiding up a relief party to a trench, recently captured, when a shell exploded and killed his officer and two comrades. The explosion of the shell rendered the bodies unrecognisable, and, as it was dark, some little doubt arose as to whether your son was in this party at the actual time; so if there is the slightest doubt in a case like this a man is reported "missing" ... I can get no definite evidence, and as he has not since been seen can only conclude that he was killed at the same time. He was a good and fearless soldier, devoted to his work, and ready to go wherever his duty called him, and his death would be greatly mourned by his comrades... I am only too sorry that I cannot hold out the hope that your son is still alive."

He is commemorated on the Thiepval Memorial, France on the Pier and Faces 5C and 12C and has no known grave. He was awarded the British War and Victory medals.

Herbert Miller
1880 – October 23 1916

Private Herbert Miller was born in Thrapston in 1880, the second oldest son. In 1881, the family lived at 23 Titchmarsh Lane (now Oundle Road). By 1891, his father had died and his mother re-married to Marshall Meadows. In both this and the 1901 census, they lived in Oundle Road. In 1901, Herbert is recorded as being a horse collar maker. Herbert was married on November 23 1910 to Olive Pitts. They had a daughter, Beatrice, born in 1912. At the time of his death, his wife was living in Warmington.

He enlisted with the Queens Royal West Surrey Regiment, 10th Battalion, Service Number G/10382, on November 6 1915 in Thrapston. He went to France on May 4 1916. As part of "D" Company he was badly wounded in the back on September 17 1916 as the Battalion moved back into support trenches near Flers, having spent the two previous days attacking enemy trenches. Between September 15 and 17, the Battalion suffered nearly 350 casualties. Herbert died of his wounds at No. 9 General Hospital, British Expeditionary Force on October 23 1916.

He was buried at St Sever Cemetery, Rouen, France with military honours in Grave B 12 18. He is commemorated on his mother's (Martha Meadows) headstone, Grave Number 182, in Oundle Road Cemetery, Thrapston along with his younger brother Walter (page 4) who died in 1914 at Poperinghe, Belgium. He was awarded the British War and Victory medals.

George Alfred Langley
1895 – October 25 1916

Private George Alfred Langley was born in 1895, the fourth child of Charles and Rosetta Langley of Denford. The 1901 census records them as living in Denford, Mr. Langley being a bricklayers labourer. After leaving school, George worked at the Smith and Grace Ironworks.

He enlisted with the 2nd Battalion Northamptonshire Regiment, Service Number 12847, in Northampton. After a period of training, he went to France on April 15 1916 and was killed in action four months into the Battle of the Somme on October 25 1916. On the day he died, the Battalion was in the trenches at Trones Wood, to the west of Guillemont. During the morning, the trenches were subjected to heavy bombardment, during which George was killed. Local papers reported his death a month later.

He is commemorated on the Thiepval Memorial, France, on the Pier and Face 11D. He has no known grave. He is recorded on the Smith and Grace Roll of Honour held at Thrapston Town Council Offices. He was awarded the 1914/1915 Star, British War and Victory medals.

George does not appear on the Memorial in Thrapston Parish Church, but is included on the Smith and Grace Roll of Honour and is also named on the Denford Memorial.

1917

Joseph George Morley..February 17 1917
Gerald Lenton...July 27 1917
William James Loaring..August 4 1917
Leonard Throssell...August 16 1917
Edward Percy Raworth..September 20 1917
John William Guest...October 7 1917
Frederick William Newman..October 8 1917
James Edward Cobley...October 21 1917
Arthur William Jeffery...November 2 1917

Joseph George Morley
1897 – February 17 1917

Private Joseph George Morley was born in 1897 at Wainfleet, Lincolnshire, the youngest of six children born to James and Eliza Morley. In 1901, the family lived at Wainfleet All Saints, Lincolnshire, where Mr. Morley was an hotel keeper. They moved to Thrapston between 1903 and 1906 where they took over the Swan Hotel. Joseph attended Kettering Grammar School, leaving in 1914. He moved to Grimsby where he worked for Barclay's Bank.

Joseph enlisted with the 6th Battalion, Northamptonshire Regiment, Service Number 27409, in August 1916 in Grimsby, Lincolnshire. He was killed in action in France on February 17 1917, when the Battalion were near Thiepval at Authville Wood in South Miraumont Trench. At 5.45am a barrage started. No further details are given in the Battalion war diary, but it is probable that Joseph was killed during this barrage. The last communication his family had from him was a field card which arrived on February 16. He had been expected to return to England in December 1917 to enter an Officers' Training Corps.

He is commemorated on the Thiepval Memorial, France, on the Pier and Face 11D. He has no known grave. He was awarded the British War and Victory medals.

A memorial service was held for him at Thrapston Parish Church on Sunday March 25 1917 and reported in the Kettering Guardian on March 30. "There was a good congregation. The hymns were "On the resurrection morning", "O God our help in ages past" and "For all the saints who from their labours rest". The Rector, the Rev. H. E. FitzHerbert, preached a very appropriate sermon from the text, "That we, being delivered out of the hands of our enemies, might serve him without fear all the days of our life". At the close of the service Miss Kingsford played the Dead March, the congregation standing".

Gerald Lenton
1883 – July 27 1917

2nd Lieutenant Gerald Lenton was born in Christchurch, Hampshire at the end of 1883, the fourth son of Henry and Lucy Lenton. Between 1887 and 1891, the family moved to Thrapston, where Mr. Lenton was the Primary School headmaster, living in Bridge Street, next to the White Hart. By 1901, Gerald had left school and was working as a pharmaceutical chemist.

He enlisted in the Honourable Artillery Company as a Private, Service Number 2780, before being commissioned to the Bedfordshire Regiment by the beginning of 1917. He joined the 2nd Battalion on February 18 1917 at Arras Trenches, Agny, France, being part of "B" Company. On March 20, at 4.30am, he took a patrol out from the line to Henin-sur-Cojeul, a village south of Arras, but returned as it was occupied. His last letter home stated that "he was in the worst shelled area in Belgium and was out with a working party every night". On July 26 1917, when the battalion was in the front lines at Zillebeke, just south of Ypres, he was wounded on a raid and died the next day. Although only with the Battalion for five months, he was described by comrades as "a fine young fellow and a gallant officer, and is spoken of in the highest terms by his brother officers and his men alike". He is buried at Lijssenthoek Military Cemetery, Belgium, in Grave Number XIV. A. 6. He was awarded the British War and Victory medals.

By the time of his death, his parents had moved to 8 Victoria Street, Hunstanton, Norfolk, and it was from there that his mother applied for his medals on August 8 1921.

Gerald is not mentioned on any of the Thrapston Rolls of Honour, but is named on the Hunstanton War Memorial and the War Memorial in St. Edmunds Church, Hunstanton.

William James Loaring
1889 – August 4 1917

William James Loaring was born in Thrapston, the son of Edwin J. & Maria Loaring. He had two brothers, Edwin George and Ernest James and two sisters, Maud G. and Ethel Mary (known as May). He was educated in Thrapston. All the boys were to enter the family business as clothiers and outfitters. To learn the trade they were sent to the East End of London to train at Spencer, Turner & Boldero, Lissom Grove, where William was at the outbreak of War in 1914. He had a regular girlfriend with whom he exchanged correspondence. Some of these letters survive.

He enlisted at Epsom, Surrey into the Royal Fusiliers, Service Number 50074, becoming a member of the 13th Battalion. He served on the Western Front in France and Flanders, his Battalion being part of the 111th Brigade which was part of the 37th Division. William was killed on August 4 1917 during an evening relief east of Messines which came under gas and artillery attack.

He is commemorated on the Menin Gate Memorial, Ypres, Panel 6 and 8. He has no known grave. He was awarded the British War and Victory medals.

He is commemorated on the panelling in St. James' Church and, as his family were members of Thrapston Baptist Church, his name is included on the church Roll of Honour.

His two brothers enlisted in the Army Service Corps and survived the war.

Leonard Throssell
April 17 1885 – August 16 1917

Private Leonard Throssell was born on April 17 1885 in Bythorn, the youngest son of Edwin and Susannah Throssell. Mr. Throssell was a farmer and cattle dealer. In 1901, his parents lived at Montague House, Chancery Lane. Leonard's whereabouts at the time of the 1901 census are unknown. He was educated at Thrapston High School under Mr. Lenton's instruction. He went to live in Canada in about 1906, working in farming, lumbering and the construction industry.

He enlisted in the Canadian Infantry 16th Battalion (Manitoba Regiment), Service Number 721342 on December 20 1915 in Winnipeg. Aged 30 on enlistment, he was unmarried, 6ft 3ins tall with grey eyes, dark hair and complexion. He returned to England in September 1916 and went to France in June 1917. He managed to return home to Thrapston for Christmas 1916, and had also been back twice in 1917, the last time being just before Easter. He was killed in action on August 16 1917 and was buried in the Maroc British Cemetery, Grenay, France in Grave Number III. M. 7. We have not been able to find the appropriate medal rolls although it is likely that he was awarded the British War and Victory medals.

At the time of his death, his mother lived in the Manor House, Chancery Lane, his father having died. Two of his brothers served with H.M. Forces during the war, both surviving.

Leonard is also commemorated in the Canadian First World War Book of Remembrance, page 339.

Edward Percy Raworth
April 1895 – September 20 1917

Rifleman Edward Percy Raworth (known to his family as Percy) was born in Thrapston in 1895, the oldest child of George and Harriet Annie Raworth. By 1901, they lived in Huntingdon Road, his Father being an iron moulder, probably at Smith and Grace. By the time of his death, the family lived in Market Road. He was educated at Thrapston, and after leaving school entered the Thrapston Post Office as a telegraph messenger. On leaving, he was presented with a walking stick by Mr. Raby (then Postmaster) and the staff. He afterwards entered the service of Sir Edward Henry, Chief Commissioner of the Metropolitan Police, and subsequently went to work at Messrs. Hitchcock and Williams, of St. Paul's Churchyard, his portrait appearing in their Roll of Honour. While in Thrapston he belonged to the Baptist Church and Sunday School.

Percy enlisted with the Rifle Brigade (The Prince Consort's Own), 11th Battalion, Service Number S/15052 at St. Paul's Churchyard, Middlesex on February 1 1916. He was killed in action on September 20 1917 at Langemark during the Third Battle of Ypres. Despite promises, their attack on enemy lines did not receive the promised smoke barrage and they came under intense artillery and machine gun fire. Of the 17 Officers and 350 Other Ranks who started the offensive, only 7 Officers and 110 men survived unscathed.

He is commemorated on the Tyne Cot Memorial, Belgium, Panel 145 – 147. He has no known grave. His medal roll card states that he was awarded only the British Victory medal, although he would have also been awarded the British War medal.

A memorial service for Percy and Private John William Guest (page 42) was held at Thrapston Baptist Church on Sunday October 28 1917.

John William Guest
October 9 1897 – October 7 1917

Private John William Guest was born in Thrapston in 1897, the fourth oldest son of John Thomas and Jessie Guest. In the 1901 census, the family lived in Huntingdon Road, Mr. Guest being a self-employed carpenter and joiner. On leaving school he entered the Post Office at Thrapston working as a telegraph messenger for some years, and then, shortly before joining up, he did duty as a postman.

He enlisted towards the end of 1914 in Huntingdon, initially in the Hunts Cyclists Battalion, Service Number 1166, later being transferred to the Machine Gun Corps 147 Company, Number 1 Section, Service Number 43194. He went to France on August 3 1916, and remained there until his death. He was killed in action on October 7 1917. His Commanding Officer wrote "We were driving back an enemy counter-attack at the time, and Guest was assisting his team commander to fire the gun, when he fell. He is my first casualty since I have been in command of this section, and he is missed by me, as well as by his comrades, for he was always cheerfully happy and bright. Only on Sunday morning when I visited him on duty I spoke to him of his bright smile, and he replied that there was no need for tears, for we were winning. It takes a brave heart to be so cheerful when standing up to the knees in mud, and with shells shrieking and whistling about all the time; and I learnt many a lesson of bravery and cheerfulness from your boy.... He is buried by the spot where he so nobly fell.... It is nice to remember that he did not die in vain, for the counter-attack was repulsed, and two days later we again advanced our line".

He is commemorated on the Tyne Cot Memorial, Belgium, Panels 154-159 and 163A. He has no known grave, his original one being obliterated by artillery fire. He was awarded the British War and Victory medals.

A memorial service for him and Rifleman Edward Percy Raworth (page 41) was held at Thrapston Baptist Church on Sunday October 28 1917.

Frederick William Newman
1882 - October 8 1917

Private Frederick William Newman, known to his family as "Benny", was born in Thrapston in 1882, the oldest son of William and Emma Newman. In 1891, he is recorded as living with his grandparents, Benjamin and Mary Newman in Bridge Street, his parents being in Woodstone, Peterborough. By 1901, he was a boarder with William and Annie Davis of Bridge Street. He worked as a fishmongers assistant for Mr. Davis. He was well known in the town, having for a number of years been ostler at the King's Arms Hotel, and formerly he was a member of the Town Football Club. He married Olive Morehen in 1915 living in Huntingdon Road. They had no children,

He enlisted originally with the Royal Sussex Regiment, Service Number 5268 on February 17 1917 in Kettering, transferring to the Machine Gun Corps, Service Number 99948. He went to France in May 1917.

He was killed in action on October 8 1917. They were leaving the front lines at Ypres when a shell burst, instantaneously killing him when a fragment of shrapnel pierced his heart.

He is buried at the Welsh Cemetery (Caesar's Nose), Belgium in Grave Number II. A. 15. He was awarded the British War and Victory medals.

A Memorial Service was held at Thrapston Baptist Church on Sunday November 4 1917 "where there was a good congregation. The choir rendered as an anthem "Abide with me," and the pastor, Rev. H. Ellis Roberts, preached from Numbers xiii 33. At the close of the service Miss Roberts played "O rest in the Lord"". As well as being remembered on the Town Roll of Honour, he is also named on the Memorial at the Baptist Church, along with his younger brother Sidney (page 61).

James Edward Cobley
1886 - October 21 1917

Lance Corporal James Edward Cobley was born in 1886 in Winwick, Huntingdonshire, the second son of George and Susan Cobley. In 1901, they lived in Bythorn, Mr. Cobley working as a horse keeper and James as a plough driver. In 1916 he married Gertrude Hall in Thrapston. Within a year she was a widow and by 1918, she had remarried to Mr. Harwell and was living in Huntingdon.

James enlisted with the Northamptonshire Regiment, 2nd Battalion, Service Number 13206, in Northampton. He went to France on April 1 1915. He was killed in action on October 21 1917 at Ploegsteert. After a Church Parade in the morning, the rest of that day was quiet. At night, a working party of 160 men went out under orders from Royal Engineers. James was one of the unfortunate men to be killed that night.

Unusually, we have been unable to find any reference to his death in local newspapers.

He is buried at Motor Car Corner Cemetery, Belgium, Grave Number B 34 and was awarded the 1914/1915 Star, British War and Victory medals.

Arthur William Jeffery
February 1898 – November 2 1917

Private Arthur William Jeffery, known as William, was born in Thrapston in 1898, the oldest son of Arthur John and Mary Elizabeth Jeffery. In 1901, the family lived in Huntingdon Road, Mr. Jeffery working as a platelayer. Before joining up he worked for Mr. D. W. David, of the Elm Farm, Thrapston. He was a great grandson of Mrs. Jarvis, of Thrapston who, at the time of his death, was in her 100th year and quite a local celebrity.

William enlisted with the Northamptonshire Regiment, 1/4th Battalion, Service Number 200963 on March 26 1915 in Thrapston. He left for Egypt on November 9 1915. He was killed in action on November 2 1917, during the Third Battle of Gaza against Turkish forces. No record for this date exists in the Battalion war diary. He was buried at the Gaza War Cemetery, Israel, in Grave Number XV. C. 1. He was awarded the 1914/1915 Star, British War and Victory medals.

By the time of his death, his parents were living at 9 Barrack Row, Islip. His official age at time of death is given as 21 years, although it is probable that he enlisted giving a false date of birth, as he was only 19 years of age when he was killed.

1918

George Johnson	March 21 1918
Alfred Shrives Loveday	March 21 1918
Septimus Leslie Ferrar	April 9 1918
Ernest Harry Mayes	April 29 1918
Horace William Reeve	May 28 1918
Thomas Barrick	June 6 1918
Frederick Bowman Angood	July 23 1918
Arthur Tarrant	August 20 1918
Robert Lewis Hiam	August 22 1918
John Thomas Stimpson	August 25 1918
Samuel Wright	September 24 1918
Ralph Buckby	September 26 1918
Sidney Newman	October 1 1918
John Rogers	October 13 1918
Arthur Randolphus Abbott	October 17 1918
George William Kenneth Smith	October 22 1918
Jonathan Booth	October 30 1918
Charles Loakes	December 4 1918
Arthur William Wright	December 4 1918

George Johnson
1896 - March 21 1918

Private George Johnson was born in Thrapston in 1896, the oldest son of Frederick William and Mary Hannah Johnson. In 1901, the family lived in Huntingdon Road, Mr. Johnson being employed as an iron moulder. George worked for Mr. Nicholls, a butcher, after leaving school. He also took ambulance certificates at local classes.

He enlisted in 1915 with the Royal Army Medical Corps, Service Number 60835 in Thrapston, and trained in Aldershot. He was part of the 8th Field Ambulance and served in Egypt and France. He had several narrow escapes whilst in France, and on one occasion volunteered to accompany an officer of another regiment to search for and bring back a man lying wounded in "No Man's Land", a dangerous task in which they were successful. He was in Thrapston on leave only a few weeks before his death. He was originally posted as "missing believed killed" in France near Arras on March 21 1918. Confirmation came later that he had died. George is recorded on the Arras Memorial, France, Bay 10. He was awarded the British War and Victory medals.

His name is also recorded on his brother's gravestone, Plot C. 67, in Oundle Road Cemetery, Thrapston.

Alfred Shrives Loveday
1898 – March 21 1918

Private Alfred Shrives Loveday was born in Thrapston in 1898, the oldest son of Harry and Emily Loveday. In 1901 they lived in Halford Street, next door to the Ferrar family. Mr. Loveday was a painter at an engineering works. After leaving school Alfred worked for two years for Colonel Benyon of Islip as a houseboy, then went to Smith and Grace as a fettler. He was a member of the Parish Church Choir for about seven years.

The story handed down through the family was that Alfred ran away from home and enlisted at the beginning of the war in Kettering, probably as an underage soldier, joining the Royal West Surrey (Queen's) Regiment, 8th Battalion, Service Number G/23748. Newspaper reports of the time suggest that he enlisted with the Queen's on February 26 1917 in Kettering and went to France in January 1918. He was killed in action on March 21 1918. The regiment had been ordered to advance and immediately came under intensive shelling. Alfred suffered a direct hit. He was posted as being "missing", presumption of death being received by his family in August 1919. His family only knew he was "missing" and it was 28 years later in 1947 that they finally heard the whole story. In 1947, Harry's grandson, Lawrence Loveday Jeffery was serving in the 3rd Battalion Grenadier Guards in Palestine and amongst his friends was a Peter Halbard from Cranford. With Peter due to go home on leave, Lawrence asked him if he would deliver a small present to his mother Mabel. Shortly afterwards Peter and his father went to Thrapston to pass on the present, and Mr. Halbard Senior's attention was drawn to a formal portrait of a young man in uniform, and asked who he was. On being told he said that he had served with him when he was killed and the above story was related.

Alfred is commemorated on the Pozieres Memorial, France on Panel 15. He has no known grave. He was awarded the British War and Victory medals.

Septimus Leslie Ferrar
1898 - April 9 1918

Gunner Septimus Leslie Ferrar, known as Leslie, was born in 1898, the youngest son of Septimus and Eliza Ferrar. In 1901, the family lived in Halford Street, Mr. Ferrar being employed as a furnace labourer. In 1909 he is recorded on the admission list to the Top School on Huntingdon Road. He was described in the local press as "a bright lad of a happy disposition, and was much liked". On leaving school he was apprenticed to Mr. A. Barnett, a Thrapston coachbuilder.

He enlisted in the Royal Field Artillery on January 18 1915 in Thrapston, when he was only just 16 years old, Service Number 82386. He was part of B Battery, 286th Brigade when he was killed on April 9 1918 aged 19 in France.

On April 9 1918, during the Battle of Estaires, the first of the Battles of the Lys, the village of Fleurbaix was subject to a massive German assault. A comrade wrote to Leslie's parents "Leslie volunteered to take a message to our headquarters. He got a cycle and made off. A few minutes afterwards the enemy were on us, so he must have been taken prisoner". He was never seen again. In mid- June 1919, his parents were advised by the War Office that as Leslie had been "missing" since April 9 1918, his death on that date had been officially presumed. His two brothers, Charles and Frederick, who enlisted with the Life Guards and Queens Royal West Surrey Regiments respectively, survived the war.

He is buried at Rue-David Military Cemetery, Fleurbaix, France in Grave Number III. G. 11. He was awarded the British War and Victory medals.

Ernest Harry Mayes
1893 - April 29 1918

Gunner Ernest Harry Mayes was born in Thrapston in 1893, the second son of Frederick and Eliza Mayes. In 1901 the family lived in Halford Street, Mr. Mayes working as a tailor. On leaving school, Ernest worked for Mr. Hensman, grocer in Bridge Street. He also attended the Thrapston Institute.

He enlisted with the Royal Field Artillery Territorial Force on September 13 1915 in Thrapston, Service Number 895761, but was in this country until September 1917, when he left for France. He was injured in September 1917, receiving an injury to his hand when a shell exploded nearby, killing the Officer with him. He was killed in action on April 29 1918 at Amiens. The family first heard the news when they received a letter from one of Ernest's comrades. Bombardier P. Lawton wrote "I borrowed an entrenching tool of the infantry and buried him as well as any man could. To me your son was a very good pal in England, and your loss has every sympathy from one who knew him so well…. Everyone who knew him held the highest regard for him. He died a death I want to have – sudden. It was plain to see that he died like a man, in the defence of Amiens".

His body was re-interred at Adelaide Cemetery, Villes-Bretonneux, France, Grave Number II. Q. 2 after the war. He is also said to have been named on the Thrapston Institute Roll of Honour. He was awarded the British War and Victory medals.

Horace William Reeve
July 3 1899 – May 28 1918

Rifleman Horace William Reeve, known to his family as Willie, was born in Banbury, Oxfordshire in 1899, the second child. His parents were William and Sophia Reeve of 3 Church Court, Banbury, Oxfordshire. By 1901 the family lived at 14 Chapel Square, Midland Road, Nuneaton, Warwickshire, Mr. Reeve working as a general labourer at the "Filter Beds". On this census return, Horace is named Willie. By 1911, Mr. Reeve had died and Mrs. Reeve and her five sons and two daughters were living at The Green, Great Staughton, near St. Neots, Cambridgeshire. Charles, the oldest, was a farm labourer. It is estimated that Willie moved to Thrapston in about 1916.

He enlisted in the Rifle Brigade 2nd Battalion in Kettering, probably in early 1917. Details of his military service are unknown.

At the end of May 1918, the British forces found themselves facing an overwhelming German attack which, despite fierce opposition, pushed the Allies back across the Aisne to the Marne in the Soissons Sector. There were 15,000 fatal casualties, Willie being one of them. He died on May 28 1918.

He is commemorated on the Soissons Memorial and has no known grave. He was awarded the British War and Victory medals. Sadly, it seems that these were never handed to his family, as there is a note on his medal card requesting permission to dispose of them.

We have been unable to find any reference to him in local newspapers.

Willie is named on the World War 1 Medal Role at the National Archives, Kew, London as William Horace in WO 372/16.

Thomas Barrick
1887 – June 6 1918

Sapper Thomas Barrick was born in Northampton in 1887, the youngest son of John and Sarah Ann Barrick. Within four years, Mr. Barrick had died and Sarah remarried to William Clayson in 1891. Thomas cannot be found on the 1891 census, but in 1901 he was living with his maternal aunt and uncle in Regent Street, Northampton. He worked as a "Rough Stuff Boy" in a Shoe Factory. Between 1911 and enlisting in 1915, he moved to Thrapston, living on High Street working as an iron moulder. By this time, his sister Kate had married and their mother Sarah was living with her at 169 Wellingborough Road, Northampton.

Thomas enlisted in Northampton on September 10 1915, initially with the Royal Engineers, Service Number T/3124. His moulding skills were tested on October 8 1915 and February 26 1916 when he was classified as Proficient and Skilled respectively. He returned home, probably engaged on war work until September 16 1917 when he was called up and joined the Durham Light Infantry, Service Number 76667 briefly before returning to the Royal Engineers, Service Number 526109 on October 14 1917. He remained in Depot until February 18 1918 when he joined 94th Field Company and shortly after went to France. He was killed in action on June 6 1918. He was buried at Marfaux British Cemetery, France in Grave No VII. H. 6.

After his death, personal effects – two letters and two photographs were returned to his sister Kate along with the British War and Victory medals which were awarded to Thomas. These were to be passed to Sarah, his mother, "in the event of her mental recovery".

Thomas is not named on any Thrapston Roll of Honour.

Frederick Bowman Angood
1882 - July 23 1918

Private Frederick Bowman Angood was born at Mepal, Cambridgeshire in 1882, the son of Frederick and Jane Angood. His father was a blacksmith and farrier. Frederick served his apprenticeship in shoemaking in St. Ives, Cambridgeshire and by 1901, he was living in Raunds, lodging with Harry and Edith Bamford in Spencer Street, working as a shoemaker. In 1912 he married Lillian Kirby, the daughter of Mr. and Mrs. James Kirby of Horton House, Thrapston. They lived in Park Road, Raunds and had two children. Before enlisting, Frederick worked for Messrs. Hall and Tebbutt, shoemakers of Raunds.

He enlisted with the Middlesex Regiment, Service Number G/86194 on August 2 1917, serving in the 19th Battalion.

He was killed on July 23 1918. His wife received a letter on July 27 from his Commanding Officer notifying her of his death "caused by a shell". Official confirmation from the War Office was received on August 4 1918. He was buried at Lijssenthoek Military Cemetery, Poperinge, Belgium, Grave Number XXVIII. G. 12. He was awarded the British War and Victory medals.

Frederick is not named on the Roll of Honour in St. James' Church, but is included on the Baptist Church Roll of Honour. He is also commemorated on the War Memorials in Raunds and Mepal, Cambridgeshire.

Arthur Tarrant
1890 - August 20 1918

Private Arthur Tarrant was born in Woodford in 1890, the youngest of six children born to Thomas and Julia Tarrant. Mr. Tarrant worked as a joiner. By 1901, the family lived in High Street, Denford. On leaving school, Arthur worked for Mr. Pettit, a Thrapston-based builder. Arthur was a member of Denford Football Club.

He enlisted with the Northamptonshire Regiment, Service Number 39912 in Kettering on February 6 1917, and served in the $1/4^{th}$ Battalion. Two days after enlisting, whilst training at Woolwich, London, he was admitted to hospital for an emergency operation. He went to Egypt in November 1917. The picture was taken locally and shows him on a camel, with antiquities in the background.

He was admitted to hospital in Kantara, Egypt in July with scabrous. He wrote to his parents on July 30 in which he stated that he was in the best of health, and expected to leave the hospital and to go up into the lines to rejoin his regiment. Shortly after writing, he developed pneumonia and died on August 20 1918. On that day, his comrades were based at Fejja. The War Diary reports "A quiet day".

He was buried in the Kantara War Memorial Cemetery, Egypt, in Grave Number D. 158. He was awarded the British War and Victory medals.

A Memorial Service was held for him in Thrapston Parish Church on September 8 1918.

Robert Lewis Hiam
December 1898 - August 22 1918

Private Robert Lewis Hiam was born in 1898 in Thrapston, the oldest son of Henry and Matilda Hiam. In 1901, they lived at the White Hart, Backway, Mr. Hiam working as an iron moulder. He attended the Thrapston Church of England School and on leaving school, completed his apprenticeship with Mr. Barnett, local coachbuilder, and then went on to work for Messrs. Mullins of Northampton. He had some musical ability which he used as a member of both the Parish Church Choir and as a cornet player in the Thrapston Silver Prize Band. He also won prizes for carving. By 1918, his parents had moved to Market Road.

Robert enlisted initially with the Army Service Corps, Service Number 300505, in Kettering, then transferred to the 1/22nd Battalion of the London Regiment (The Queens), Service Number G/67076 on March 12 1917, leaving for France in February 1918.

He was killed by machine gun fire on August 22 1918, during a British attack to recapture Albert and the road between Albert and Bray-sur-Somme. His Commanding Officer later wrote to his parents "...how sorry we all were to lose poor Hiam. Always a cheerful, willing lad, he was quite a promising young soldier, and his death was a distinct loss to his company. He was killed by a machine gun bullet in our attack on August 22nd, and was buried near where he fell."

He is buried at Bray Military Cemetery, France, Grave Number II. J. 22. He was awarded the British War and Victory medals.

John Thomas Stimpson
October 20 1883 - August 25 1918

Private John Thomas Stimpson was born in Kettering in 1883, the oldest son of John and Lucy Stimpson. By 1891, they lived in Church Villas, Chancery Lane, Mr. Stimpson working as an iron moulder. After leaving school, John worked as a hairdresser. He married Elsie Kathleen Harris in Thrapston in 1907, and they had three children, Florence, Doris and John. He moved to Ramsey, Cambridgeshire just before signing up in early 1915.

He enlisted in the 3/1st Hunts Cyclists Battalion, Service Number 1360 in Huntingdon on May 14 1915, before transferring to the Royal Fusiliers, Service Number 295291, and served in the 2/4th (City of London) Battalion. He went to France on August 1 1917 and was wounded in the left thigh on September 20 1917. He returned to France in January 1918. He wrote many letters to his family from the trenches, which are in the possession of his descendents.

He was killed in action on August 25 1918 at Billow Wood near Bronfay with 13 of his comrades. He is buried at Bronfay Farm Military Cemetery, Bray-sur-Somme, France in Grave Number II. F. 22. He was awarded the British War and Victory medals.

John is commemorated on the Ramsey War Memorial, Cambridgeshire and also on his wife's (Elsie Kathleen Perkins) headstone at Grave Number 1551, Oundle Road Cemetery, Thrapston. At the time of his death she was living in Midland Road Thrapston.

Note – John's City of London Battalion Service Number is given as 295791by the Commonwealth War Graves Commission. His Medal Card gives 295291 – this is the one quoted above as being the most contemporaneous.

Samuel Wright
1889 - September 24 1918

Lance Sergeant Samuel Wright was born in Thrapston in 1889, the third son of Henry and Ann Wright. In 1891, the family lived in Titchmarsh Lane (now Oundle Road), Mr. Wright working as a chimney sweep. They were at the same address in 1901. On leaving school, Samuel worked for a local bootmaker, Mr. Barnard of Bridge Street.

He enlisted with the Northamptonshire Regiment in Northampton in about 1905, Service Number 8539, remaining with them until his transfer to the Leicestershire Regiment 1st Battalion, Service Number 43295, during the latter part of the war. He first went to France in November 1914. He married Emmie May Reason in Colchester in 1915, setting up home in Thrapston.

After surviving almost four years of conflict, he was killed in action regaining the villages of Caulaincourt and Trefcon, near St. Quentin, France on September 24 1918.

He is buried in Trefcon British Cemetery, Caulaincourt, France, Grave Number C. 61. He was awarded the 1914 Star and Clasp, British War and Victory medals.

Ralph Buckby
1895 - September 26 1918

Second Lieutenant Ralph Buckby was born in Kettering in 1895, the only son of Harry and Mary Buckby of Burton Latimer. In 1901, the family lived in Kettering Road, Burton Latimer, Mr. Buckby working as a shoe riveter. After leaving school, Ralph worked as an engineer and was with Smith and Grace prior to joining up at the onset of war.

Ralph enlisted in the Northamptonshire Regiment on September 3 1914, being attached to the Army Service Corps (Motor Transport), Service Number 162165. He was also in the Royal Army Medical Corps and was mentioned in dispatches on December 13 1915. He was subsequently transferred behind the lines to follow his trade as an engineer in the repair shop. He was discharged from the Army on July 21 1918 and commissioned into the Royal Air Force, being gazetted on July 22 1918. Shortly after, he went to France and joined 99 Squadron. He flew on raids on August 22, 23 and 25 and September 2, 3 and 15. His final raid was on September 26 1918, flying a De Havilland 9, number E632. The Pilot was Lieutenant Stanley Gilbert, Ralph being the Observer. The aeroplane was shot down behind German lines, near the French Communities of St. Ruffine and Moulin-les-Metz. Ralph was buried in Moulin Les Metz Commune Cemetery, whilst Lieutenant Gilbert was interred at St. Ruffine Commune Cemetery, the only War Graves in each. He was awarded the 1914/1915 Star, British War & Victory medals.

Ralph is not mentioned on the Rolls of Honour in St James' or the Baptist Church, but is included on the Smith and Grace Roll of Honour. He is also commemorated on the Burton Latimer Memorial.

Sidney Newman
January 6 1897 - October 1 1918

Private Sidney Newman was born in Thrapston on January 6 1897, the youngest son of William and Emily Newman of Huntingdon Road. In 1901, the family lived at the same address, Mr. Newman working as a bricklayer. Sidney worked for Messrs. Heighton, Thrapston, as a driver and mechanic.

He enlisted in 1916 in Northampton. After a short time in the Army Service Corps Transport Section, Service Number 268477, he transferred to the York and Lancaster Regiment, 6th (Service) Battalion, Service Number 33724 and went to France in January 1917. He was killed in action on October 1 1918 near Epinoy. The attack on a railway embankment commenced at 5.00am and resulted in very heavy casualties, the enemy strength having been badly underestimated. No ground was gained.

As well as being on the St. James' Roll of Honour, he is mentioned alongside his brother Frederick, who was killed in Belgium a year earlier (page 43), on the Roll of Honour in the Baptist Church. He is commemorated on the Vis-en-Artois Memorial, France on Panel 9. He has no known grave. He was awarded the British War and Victory medals.

John James Rogers
1894 - October 13 1918

Gunner John James Rogers was born in Sharnbrook, Bedfordshire in 1894. In 1901 he lived with his parents at the grocers shop, Yelden, Bedfordshire. His parents are named as William and Elizabeth Clark. Whether Mrs. Clark had remarried is currently unknown. John moved to Thrapston in about 1912, probably living with his uncle, Mr. John Coleman of Market Road. He worked for Mr. Hensman for three years, then at the furnaces, probably Islip. He was an enthusiastic bellringer at St. James Church.

He enlisted on November 9 1915 in Thrapston with the Royal Field Artillery Territorial Force, Service Number 891544. He served in Mesopotamia, then in France. He was wounded in the back whilst servicing the guns, and died shortly afterwards of his wounds on October 13 1918. His Commanding Officer wrote to John's mother "He was a good fellow, and one of our best gunners. He was serving the guns when he was wounded in the back. He took it like a hero, and five minutes afterwards was laughing and joking and quite in good spirits when he went off to hospital, and everybody was very sorry and surprised when the news came through that he had died. What he was like after he left the battery I don't know, but from what I can gather he suffered very little. I am sure his death must be a very great loss to you, and I tender my very deepest sympathy".
He was buried at Delsaux Farm Cemetery, Beugny, France, Grave Number I. E. 21. He was awarded the British War and Victory medals.

By the time of his death, his Mother was living in Swineshead, Bedfordshire.

As a mark of respect, the Thrapston Bellringers rang, with bells half muffled, 720 Oxford Bob and 360 Plain Bob. He is remembered in the The Central Council Memorial Book of Church Bell-Ringers Who Fell in the Great War 1914-1918 in St. Paul's Cathedral, London, on page 24.

Arthur Randolphus Abbott
October 10 1899 - October 17 1918

Signalman Arthur Randolphus Abbott was born on October 10 1899, the third child and second son of Horace and Ellen Abbott. The family lived in Market Road, Mr. Abbott being employed as an iron moulder. Arthur was admitted to Thrapston Council School in 1909. After leaving school, he was apprenticed with Mr. Glenn, hairdresser of Bridge Street. He was a good singer and performed in local concerts.

He joined the Royal Navy on October 12 1915, Service Number J45512. After service on HMS Impregnable he was transferred to the "Ganges" at Harwich on February 18 1916. He then went to the naval barracks at Chatham. Towards the end of 1916, he joined the "Proserpine" training ship in the Persian Gulf, where he finished his training. He served in several ships, the last being the "Dalhousie". He developed tuberculosis whilst stationed in Bombay, India. He returned to Britain for treatment and convalescence at Gosport, Hampshire. He did not respond and, after being discharged from the Navy on July 4 1918, had a short stay at home before moving to Ipswich Sanatorium for ten weeks. Treatment was not successful and he returned home to Thrapston on October 2 1918. His condition deteriorated and he died at home on October 17 1918, one week after his nineteenth birthday.

After a funeral service at the Baptist Church, he was buried in the Oundle Road Cemetery, Grave Number 980. As well as personal details, his Gravestone also carries the verse – "Safe at last the harbour passed, Safe in his father's home." Arthur was awarded the British War and Victory medals.

He is commemorated on both the St James' and Baptist Church Rolls of Honour.

George William Kenneth Smith
May 20 1899 - October 22 1918

Lieutenant George William Kenneth Smith was born on May 20 1899, the only son of Mr. and Mrs. Theodore Smith of Orchard House, Thrapston. He was educated at Eaglehurst College, Northampton and, on leaving school, entered the Bedford Branch of the Northamptonshire Union Bank. His Service Record states that he worked for Smith and Grace between February 1916 and May 1917. He is not named on the Company Roll of Honour.

He joined the Royal Flying Corps at the end of May 1917. During the summer of 1918, he gave the inhabitants of Thrapston a flying display which was so impressive, it was described in his obituary as being "clever". He was transferred to serve in France on August 14 1918. His Service Record gives no indication of Squadron.

In a letter written on October 8, he mentioned that he had been flying at dawn. Later that day, he was admitted to the 3rd Australian Clearing Station dangerously ill with wounds to his neck. He had been shot in the neck whilst flying yet had managed to fly his plane 30 miles back to base and landed safely. On October 15, letters were received from Lieut. Smith stating that he was going on splendidly, which encouraged the hope that he was progressing favourably and would recover. He died on October 22 1918 of his wounds. The family heard of his death by telegram on October 28 stating "Report just received states that Lieut. Smith died of wounds on October 22nd".

He is buried at Terlincthun British Cemetery, Wimille, France in Grave Number VI. B. 24. He was awarded the British War and Victory medals.

Jonathan Booth
October 23 1889 - October 30 1918

Trooper Jonathan Booth, sometimes known as Jack, was born in Thrapston in 1889, the seventh child and third son of Obadiah and Harriet Booth. The family lived in Titchmarsh Lane (now Oundle Road). Mr. Booth was a glass and china dealer and also a fireman. For many years, he was the Captain of the Town Fire Brigade. Jonathan worked for Lieutenant Colonel Benyon, of Islip House, for eight years as a groom. He then worked in the local Ironstone Mines. He was a member of Thrapston Football Club and, for two years, was a member of the Fire Brigade.

He enlisted early in 1915 in Northampton with the Northamptonshire Yeomanry, B Squadron, 1/1st Battalion, Service Number 146036. After service in France, he went to Italy, where he was killed in action on October 30 1918 near Sacile. He was with an advanced patrol and, with a corporal, got under a farmhouse. A machine gun was in the farmhouse, and, opening fire, frightened the horses. Jack's horse got away from him, and in trying to secure it he came under fire and was shot through the heart. He was buried next day by two of his comrades, after the farm had been taken, and a cross was erected over his grave. His Commanding Officer was the same Colonel Benyon from Islip he had worked for before the War. He was reburied at Giavera British Cemetery, Arcade, Italy in Grave Number 6. K. 9. He was awarded the British War and Victory medals.

Jonathan is not recorded on the oak panelling in St. James' Church. This was at the express wish of his father.

Charles Loakes
1882 - December 4 1918

Private Charles Loakes was born in 1882 in Great Addington, the second son of Joseph Chapman and Elizabeth Loakes. He spent his childhood in the village. By 1891 he was staying with his grandmother, Hannah Loakes. The family lived in West Side Street, Great Addington, Mr. Loakes working as an agricultural labourer. Elizabeth Loakes died in 1897. Charles married Margaret Mary Bailey in Thrapston in 1909 and they lived in Woodford until 1915, when they moved to Midland Road. They had three children. He set up the business W. and C. Loakes, Builders and Contractors, with his brother William.

Charles enlisted on February 1 1917, joining the Queen's Royal West Surrey Regiment, Service Number T/205423. He arrived in France on June 1 1917. He was wounded in the arm in March 1918. He contracted influenza and was admitted to the 57th Casualty Clearing Station, France on November 25, also suffering with pneumonia. He died on December 4 1918.

He is buried in Valenciennes (St. Roch) Communal Cemetery, France in Grave Number I. F. 39. He was awarded the British War and Victory medals.

He is also commemorated on his wife's headstone in Grave Number 227 at Oundle Road Cemetery, Thrapston.

Arthur William Wright
1893 - December 4 1918

Private Arthur William Wright was born in 1893 at Hillrow, Haddenham, Cambridgeshire, the oldest son and second child of Joseph and Rose Wright. Joseph was a labourer. The family were still in Hillrow at the 1901 census. At some point, they moved to Twywell, this being Joseph and Rose's address when Arthur died.

Arthur enlisted with the Northamptonshire Regiment, Service Number 58453, transferring to the Gloucestershire Regiment, Service Number 42453 (or 42458), being in the 1/6 Battalion. He first went to France on December 26 1915. Further details of his service are currently unknown.

He died on December 4 1918, probably of Spanish Flu. He is buried at Dueville Communal Cemetery Extension, Italy in Grave Number 2. A. 4. He was awarded the 1915 Star and British and Victory Medals.

Arthur is named in the Roll of Honour in St. James' Church but did not have his name carved on the panelling. The reason for this is unclear.

1919

John Harry Shadbolt..January 7 1919
Ernest Wilfred Barratt...February 25 1919

1921

Frederick William Johnson...January 5 1921

John Harry Shadbolt
1898 - January 7 1919

Private John Harry Shadbolt was born in Thrapston in 1898, the second son of William and Bertha Shadbolt. Mr. Shadbolt was a cycle dealer, later branching out into motor cars. They lived in Bridge Street. On leaving school, John worked in the family business.

He enlisted in April 1917, initially with the Transport Section, then the King's Royal Rifle Corps before transferring to the Machine Gun Corps, Service Number 108301. He went to Egypt at the end of 1917 where shortly after arrival, he had dysentery and a septic knee, and was in hospital for some time. Later, he was again admitted to hospital with septic poisoning.

On January 3 1919, his family received a telegram stating that he was dangerously ill with pneumonia. Confirmation of his death of pneumonia on January 7 1919 in the 3rd Echelon Hospital, Alexandria, Egypt was received on January 10. He was buried in Deir El Belah War Cemetery, Israel, Grave Number C. 42. He is commemorated on the Baptist Church Roll of Honour. He was awarded the British War and Victory medals.

A well attended Memorial Service was held for him and Ernest Wilfred Barratt (page 72) at St. James' Church on Sunday March 16 1919.

Ernest Wilfred Barratt
1895 – February 25 1919

Sapper/Private Ernest Wilfred Barratt was born in 1895 in Thurning, Northamptonshire, the second son of Henry and Mary Ann Barratt. The family moved to Thrapston at an unknown date, and lived in Market Road, Ernest working as a saddler/ harness maker.

He enlisted in Northampton on August 24 1916 with the Royal Engineers, Service Number 216136, but was not called up until December 11 1916. He transferred to the 9th Battalion North Staffordshire Regiment (Pioneer Battalion), Service Number 49946, on September 10 1917, the day he sailed to Calais. He served in the field from October 12 1917 until he returned to Britain on December 14 1918. He rejoined his Regiment on January 10 1919, but contracted influenza on February 18 1919.

He died on February 25 1919 at the 20th Casualty Clearing Station in France, of influenza. He is buried at Charleroi Communal Cemetery, Belgium, Grave Number J. 12. He was awarded the British War and Victory medals.

A memorial Service was held for him and John Harry Shadbolt (page 71) at St. James' Church on March 16 1919 which many relatives and friends attended.

Frederick William Johnson
1899 – January 5 1921

Private Frederick William Johnson was born in 1899 in Thrapston, the second son of Frederick and Hannah Johnson. In 1901, the family lived in the High Street, Mr. Johnson working as an iron moulder.

He enlisted on May 17 1916 in Northampton aged 16 years, initially in the Royal Field Artillery, Service Number 147049 before transferring to the Tank Corps, serving in the 44th Battalion, Service Number 111391. His service details are unknown, although he was said to have been through many engagements and had some narrow escapes. A medical examination on December 17 1918 diagnosed pulmonary tuberculosis, aggravated by his war service. He was awarded a War Pension of £2.00 a week on September 30 1919, reduced to £1 12s a week from December 18 1919. By August 1920, he was confined to bed. He did not make any improvement and died at the family home in Grove Road on January 5 1921. He was buried in Thrapston Cemetery, Oundle Road, Grave Number C. 67. He was awarded the British War and Victory medals.

His older brother, George Johnson (page 49), who died March 21 1918, is also named on his headstone.

The family suffered two bereavements from tuberculosis within four days – Frederick's aunt, Emma Johnson died on January 1 1921 and was buried the day after Frederick's death.

World War 2

Jack Cornwell	June 8 1940
William Charles Frank Capps	May 1 1941
Christopher Jackson	December 27 1941
Alfred William Taney	November 7 1942
Thomas James Bowyer	January 11 1943
Alfred Ernest Hodson	June 6 1943
Aubrey Ernest Cullum	July 18 1943
Robert Thomas Smith	September 9 1943
John William Hill	October 30 1943
Harold Groom	June 11 1944
Herbert Brown Wagstaff	June 25 1944
Donald Francis Barber	February 6 1945
Frank Arthur Gifford	February 17 1945
Leslie Ernest Barber	February 6 1946

Jack Cornwell
1918 – June 8 1940

Marine Jack Cornwell was born in 1918 in Thrapston, a son of Mr and Mrs A. Cornwell. He had two brothers, Oliver and Timothy and a sister Geneva.

Jack went to Huntingdon Road Council School and on leaving was employed at the Islip Furnaces.

He decided to leave the furnaces and enlist as a Royal Marine in 1936 and did so at Plymouth, his Service Number being PLY/X 2447. Several parts of the world were visited by Jack during his pre war service.

In June 1940, Jack was serving on HMS Glorious, an aircraft carrier that with its escort of destroyers, HMS Acasta and HMS Ardent, was assisting at the evacuation of British and Allied forces from Norway.

Glorious had flown on twenty RAF fighters to return to the UK, as well as ten fighters and five torpedo bombers of the Fleet Air Arm. The three British ships were intercepted by the German battlecruisers Gneisenau and Scharnhorst on Saturday June 8 in the Norwegian Sea and in a little over two hours all three British ships were sunk by gunfire with a loss of over 1500 officers and men of the Royal Navy, Royal Marines and Royal Air Force. There were only thirty nine survivors.

Jack Cornwell lost his life during this action. He has no known grave and is commemorated on the Plymouth Naval Memorial, Panel 43, Column 1.

William Charles Frank Capps
1911 – May 1 1941

Gunner William Charles Frank Capps (known as Frank), was born at Burton Latimer in 1911, he was an only child. After being educated at Thrapston Council School and then Kettering Central School he was apprenticed to the Evening Telegraph newspaper at their Thrapston office.

He was an enthusiastic newspaper reporter and also very active in promoting the district's organisations and sports clubs. He was once chairman of Thrapston Harriers and a keen supporter of Thrapston Thursday Football Club.

Frank was a member of Thrapston Town Band and regularly contributed to his paper's "County Band Notes" as "Allegro", encouraging brass bands large and small. He was also a member of the Institute of Journalists.

He married in 1936 to Miss Barbara Loveday, a Thrapston girl, and they set up home in Huntingdon Road. His parents lived at 67 Midland Road, Thrapston.

In 1940, Frank joined the Royal Artillery as a Gunner, Service Number 997420. He was serving in Yorkshire as his Battery's clerk, when after a severe chill he developed pleurisy. This resulted in his admission to Wakefield Hospital where pneumonia then set in and he unfortunately died.

Following his cremation at Leeds, the funeral service took place at St. James' Parish Church, Thrapston and he was buried at Oundle Road Cemetery in Grave Number 165.

Christopher Jackson
1919 – December 27 1941

Private Christopher Jackson was born in Thrapston the youngest son of Samuel and Edith of Halford Street. His older brother was Frank Jackson.

Chris went to Huntingdon Road Council School and was apprenticed to Loaring and Son the Thrapston outfitters, later going to Cook, Son & Co., St.Paul's Churchyard, London, EC4 where he was a popular staff member. He was a member of the Thrapston Institute.

At the beginning of the war Chris enlisted and joined the $2/7^{th}$ Battalion, The Queen's Royal Regiment (West Surrey) with Service Number 6092844. He went to France with them as part of the 35th Infantry Brigade, 12th Division in April 1940 and was engaged on lines of communication duties. When the German invasion began they were rushed up to Abbeville, but with no Artillery, Engineers or Anti-tank weapons to speak of they were quickly overrun and it was at this time that Chris Jackson was captured and became a prisoner of war.

He worked on a farm in Germany for a time and was then sent to repair roads in Poland. There he developed trouble with his left leg due to the heavy work and was sent to a hospital near Dresden in Germany and underwent an operation. While he was in the hospital Chris suffered chronic bronchitis and pleurisy set in. Pneumonia developed and as a result Chris died. He was originally buried in the churchyard behind Konigswartha Hospital.

After the war he was reinterred in the Berlin 1939 – 1945 War Cemetery, Germany, Plot 11, Grave M7.

Alfred William Taney
1915 – November 7 1942

Sergeant Pilot Alfred William Taney was born in Oundle in 1915 the only son of Harry and Edith Taney. His father had been the Chief Officer of the Fire Brigade there.

Alfred was educated at Oundle Council School, the Laxton Grammar School and Oundle School, qualifying well for a place at Chester College. He played both cricket and football for his college as he had done for his schools. Athletics was another sport that he enjoyed.

He left college a qualified teacher and his first post was at Earls Barton where he remained for four years. His next appointment was at Enfield in north London.

Some time before the war, Alfred's parents moved to Thrapston and when the war commenced Harry Taney became a Company Officer in the National Fire Service. Alfred was married in 1940 to Miss Annie Booth of Leeds.

Alfred joined the Royal Air Force in 1941, with Service Number 1206121 and was sent to Rhodesia for his flying training. He returned home in the autumn of 1942 and was posted to various stations.

On November 7 1942 on returning from a night operation Alfred's aeroplane crashed and he was killed.

The funeral took place in Leeds and he is buried in Leeds (Lawns Wood) Cemetery, Section X, Grave 202.

Thomas James Bowyer
1922 – January 11 1943

Trooper Thomas James Bowyer was born in 1922 at Jessamine House, High Street, Buckden, Huntingdonshire, the eldest son of William and Mabel Bowyer, farmers. His younger brothers were William and John (known as Jack).

After preparatory school at Cedar House, St. Neots, Tom went to Kimbolton School as a boarder and when he left aged fifteen, he went to work for Bletsoe's at Thrapston with the intention of becoming an auctioneer. He lodged in Thrapston during the week and cycled home to his parents at the weekends.

Tom was a good artist and keen on playing tennis. He also liked to go ferreting with his brothers.

During the early days of the war he was keen to join up and although not old enough he sought to be released from his job and managed to join the 13th Battalion, Sherwood Foresters (Notts. and Derby. Regiment) Service Number 4983194. This unit was converted into 163rd Regiment, Royal Armoured Corps which formed part of the short lived 267th Indian Tank Brigade in India July 1942 and was disbanded in April 1943. It was to have served in the Burma Campaign.

Anxious to serve overseas, Tom went out to India in the autumn of 1942 and a few months later caught meningitis from which he sadly died.

Tom was buried in Trimulghery No.12 Military Cemetery, India, Plot B, Grave No.1548. In 1953 his remains were moved to Madras War Cemetery, Plot VIII, Grave B16.

Alfred Ernest Hodson
December 15 1907 – June 6 1943

Leading Aircraftsman Alfred Ernest Hodson was born at Woodford, Northamptonshire in 1907 the third son of Alfred and Louisa. He had three brothers, Horace, Percy and Kenneth and a sister, Linda.

The family moved to Thrapston and lived in Huntingdon Road. Alfred was educated at Thrapston CE School and also attended St. James' Sunday School and was awarded a prize book in 1919 by the Rector H.E. Fitzherbert. He became a hairdresser, eventually owning two salons, one at Buckden and the other at Brampton, both in Huntingdonshire.

He married Phyllis May Garratt on January 12 1931 and had one son, Anthony Arthur. They lived at Salome Wood Farm Cottage at Hammerton.

In 1941 Alfred joined the Royal Air Force Volunteer Reserve with Service Number 1045770 and was stationed at RAF Topcliffe in Yorkshire. He was promoted to Leading Aircraftsman in July 1942.

He was then posted to North Africa, disembarking in November 1942, serving with the 109 RSU (Repair and Servicing Unit).

Alfred was involved in an accident on June 6 1943 and died as a result of his injuries. His family say that after visiting a friend in hospital he was struck by an ambulance.

He is buried in the Bone War Cemetery, Annaba, Algeria, Plot IV, Grave E9.

Aubrey Ernest Cullum
August 31 1921 – July 18 1943

Trooper Aubrey Ernest Cullum was born in 1921 at "Springfield", Oundle Road, Thrapston, the second son of Henry and Eliza, the other boys were Stanley, James and Reginald.

Aubrey went to Titchmarsh School from 1925 and after a move to Leighton Bromswold, returned and finished his education at Thrapston's Huntingdon Road School. He then went to work for Mr W. Watts, a grocer of Kettering.

In January 1942 he joined the 44th Royal Tank Regiment, R.A.C. Service Number 7949643 and in July went overseas to serve with them in North Africa. It was reported in the "Thrapston, Raunds and Oundle Journal" in October 1942 that he had met up with two other Thrapston lads, Johnny Thurlow and Ken Shipton, and were having a good time together.

On July 10 1943, Aubrey landed in Sicily at Avola with his Regiment and they fought their way north towards Catania. It was vital to capture and hold the Primasole Bridge over the Simeto River intact and it was during the fierce fighting to achieve this on July 18 that Aubrey's tank, commanded by Sergeant McGann of C Squadron, was hit by mortar fire and knocked out. Aubrey was killed and two other men were wounded, one of which, Hugh Bishop, was later killed in Italy on December 6, 1943.

Aubrey is buried in Catania War Cemetery, Sicily, Plot II, Grave C37.and also named upon Titchmarsh War Memorial.

After the war Denis Knight of the 44th RTR wrote a poem in memory of his fallen comrades called "Let not those kind F-words be lost" in which Aubrey and others are mentioned. This poem can be found on page 121.

Robert Thomas Smith
1916 – September 9 1943

Bombardier Robert Thomas Smith was born in Kettering in 1916, the oldest son of Mr. and Mrs. S. Smith of Alfred Street, Kettering. He had two brothers and a sister.

Bob was educated at St. Andrew's School in Kettering and after worked as a clicker for Loake Brothers, a well-known firm of Kettering shoemakers.

He married Kathleen Parker and had a daughter. They lived in Washington Street, Thrapston. (now Highfield Road). His interests included angling (he belonged to several Kettering clubs) and football.

Bob enlisted in the army in April 1940, joining the 142 (Royal North Devon Yeomanry) Field Regiment, Royal Artillery with Service Number 976170. They were part of the country's defence forces and were to be equipped with the "Bishop" self-propelled gun. This was a 25pdr gun mounted on a Valentine tank chassis. In July 1943 the Regiment was sent to Sicily and saw a lot of action.

During his time in Sicily the press interviewed Bob and an article appeared in the Thrapston, Raunds and Oundle Journal in August 1943 under the title "Gallivanting Gunner from Thrapston" (page 122).

The Regiment was then required for the landings at Salerno, in Italy. Bob was a commander of a "Bishop" in E Troop, 506 Battery which was loaded onto a tank landing craft LCT 572. The convoy set off and at 3.25am on September 9 the LCT struck a mine and sank, taking with it the "Bishops" of E Troop and fourteen of the men, one of whom was Bob. His body was recovered by a US ship and then buried at sea.

He is commemorated at the Cassino Memorial, Italy, on Panel 2.

John William Hill
1915 – October 30 1943

Corporal John William Hill was born in 1915, the second son of John Henry and Esther Hill. After his schooling in Thrapston he went to work at the Islip Furnaces as a furnace labourer.

He was married to Dorothy May and they lived at Washington Street (now Highfield Road), Thrapston.

As a reservist, John was called up at the outbreak of the War into the 2nd Battalion, Northamptonshire Regiment with Service Number 5882457. He saw service in France and was evacuated from Dunkirk in 1940. His battalion went to Madagascar and after that he served in India, Sicily and Italy as part of the 17th Brigade attached to the British 5th Infantry Division.

John's Battalion fought up into central Italy to the north of Naples in the area of the Matese Mountains encountering stiff opposition. Enemy shelling was effective and it was impossible to dig into the hard ground. The only means of protection was to build sangar-like shelters as was done on the north-west frontier of India. By October 31 the 2nd Northamptons had captured the village of Macchiagodena at the cost of several casualties, including the death of Corporal John Hill on October 30.

John is buried at the Cassino War Cemetery, Italy, Plot VII, Grave A8.

Harold Groom
1916 – June 11 1944

Lance Corporal Harold Groom was born in 1916, a son of John and Kate Groom of Midland Road, Thrapston. He had a sister, Mary and two brothers, Tom and Arthur.

Harold was educated at Thrapston Huntingdon Road School and went to work as an electrician for Grensell Electrical Contractors of Kettering.

He was a keen cricketer and was at one time secretary of Denford Cricket Club.

In May1940 Harold joined the Royal Army Service Corps and served in Egypt. When the Royal Electrical and Mechanical Engineers was formed in October 1942, Harold transferred, with his Service Number 190878, to this new unit.

While in Egypt, he broadcast a message to his parents from Alexandria and also met up with his brother Tom, who was serving with the Royal Engineers and his brother in law Denis Webb from Raunds.

Harold was killed in Italy on June 11 1944 and is buried in Naples War Cemetery, Plot I, Grave O 11.

Herbert Brown Wagstaff
1916 – June 25 1944

Gunner Herbert Brown "Bert" Wagstaff was born at Thorpe Waterville in 1916. He went to Thrapston Church of England School and on leaving worked for Mr W. Fletton of Thorpe Achurch.

Bert left to join Sainsbury's and worked at several of their London branches. He came to Kettering shortly after a new branch opened there. Later on he worked for the Prudential Assurance, operating the Marston district of Bedfordshire.

Being a very keen cyclist, Bert assisted in the formation of Thrapston Cycling Club taking part in many time trials. He also ran for Thrapston and District Harriers.

As a boy he played football for the successful Thrapston Crusaders, also playing for Sainsbury's in his London days. He enjoyed any form of sporting activity and was a member of the Thrapston Institute. He married Ivy Mary Marsh and they lived in Halford Street, Thrapston.

Bert enlisted and joined the 55 Light Anti-Aircraft Regiment, Royal Artillery, Service Number 1525302. The Regiment was sent to India and in September 1943 was converted into 55 AA/Anti-Tank Regiment, comprising two Anti-Aircraft and two Anti-Tank Batteries. The Regiment was attached to the 20th Indian Division and sent into Burma to try and halt the Japanese advance. After desperate fighting the 20th Indian Division fell back towards Imphal.

On June 22 the Division, along with Bert's Regiment, moved out to clear the town of Ukhrul of Japanese and to join up with the approaching Chindit Brigade. It was during attacks on June 25 that Bert was killed in action.

He is buried at Imphal War Cemetery, Burma, Plot 4, Grave E17.

Donald Francis Barber
1922 – February 6 1945

Warrant Officer Donald Francis Barber was born in Thrapston in 1922. He was the second son of John and Beatrice Barber, who were fruiterers in the High Street, where they lived over the shop. Around 1927 the family moved to Oundle, where the family business was to carry on.

Don had an older brother Leslie and two younger sisters Daphne and Isobel. He was educated in Oundle and married Averil Eileen.

When the war began, as soon as he was able, he joined the Royal Air Force Volunteer Reserve, Service Number 1216829. The RAF sent him to Canada for his pilot training. On completion, he was posted to Transport Command.

On February 6 1945, whilst flying with his navigator Flight Sergeant John Coleman of Peterborough, the aeroplane encountered difficulties and as a result crashed, killing both men. They had flown together since Don's return from Canada and were close friends. Their parents being aware of this, wished for their sons to be buried along side each other in Oundle Cemetery.

The double funeral with full military honours took place at Oundle Parish Church on Saturday February 10 1945. Both coffins were draped with the Union Jack and borne by six NCOs and men of the Royal Air Force.

He is commemorated on the Oundle War Memorial.

Tragically a year to the day later Don's older brother Leslie (page 90) was killed in North Africa where he was serving with the Cheshire Regiment.

Frank Arthur Gifford
1901 – February 17 1945

Private Frank Arthur Gifford was born in 1901, the eldest son of Frank and Harriet Gifford, who farmed at Old Weston, Huntingdonshire.

He left Thrapston at an early age and after his education worked for the firm of I & R Morley of London, who were drapers. They were evacuated during the war to Nottingham.

Frank married Daisy Asplen in 1921 and they had three children.

During World War Two Frank joined the army and served with the Royal Army Pay Corps with Service Number 14260108. He was stationed in the U.K.

He died at Nottingham following discharge from a Military Hospital.

After the funeral he was buried in Thrapston Cemetery, Oundle Road, Grave Number 181.

Leslie Ernest Barber
1919 – February 6 1946

Private Leslie Ernest Barber was born in Thrapston in 1919, the eldest son of John and Beatrice Barber, fruiterers, who lived over their shop in the High Street. Les had a very serious accident when he was about four years old and needed many operations over a number of years. These left him with a metal plate over part of his skull and a right leg that was under developed.

The family moved to Oundle around 1927, where a new shop was opened. With his education completed he went to work in the family business. He did not take to this and went to work at the Smith and Grace Iron Foundry at Midland Road, Thrapston, lodging in Halford Street. Some of his leisure time was taken up with being a drummer in the Cyril Diamond Dance Band.

Les joined the army in July 1940 with the Leicestershire Regiment and due to his level of fitness he was transferred into the Cheshire Regiment with Service number 4864703. His war service was guarding Prisoners of War, firstly on the Isle of Man and from 1943 in North Africa. The monotony of his work encouraged him to form a dance band for the recreation of his comrades and great efforts were made to obtain the necessary instruments.

He married a Thrapston girl, Joan Bamford and they had a daughter, Christine, who was six months old when he last saw her.

Tragedy struck on February 6 1946, only a few weeks before his demobilisation. Les was a passenger in an army lorry travelling in North Africa when it was involved in an accident, resulting in him being killed.

He is buried in Dely Ibrahim War Cemetery, Algeria, Plot 2 Grave J8.

Iraq

Stephen James Edwards...2007

Stephen James Edwards
October 11 1971 – July 31 2007

Corporal Stephen James Edwards was born on October 11 1971, the second son of Mr and Mrs Alan Edwards of Thrapston. He was educated at Thrapston Primary School, The King John Middle School and Prince William at Oundle. His older brother, Paul, is also in the army and a senior NCO.

Steve started work as an apprentice agricultural engineer at Rustons and when that company closed he was employed at the Smith and Grace works in Midland Road, Thrapston, where he was able to complete his studies.

He decided to join the army and did so in June 1993, entering the 2nd Royal Tank Regiment, with Service Number 25026852. His initial training took place at Winchester and Catterick, where he was to achieve "Top Soldier".

On being posted to his regiment Steve saw service all around the world, notably in Canada, Northern Ireland, Cyprus, the Balkans, the Arabian Gulf and Iraq. He had been promoted to the rank of Corporal and was a tank commander. The regiment was stationed at Sennelager in Germany and there Steve was to meet his wife Gabi and they were to have their son, Ryan.

During the recent Iraq War, Steve had been in the country since early May 2007 as a member of Badger Squadron of 2nd Royal Tank Regiment, attached to the Irish Guards Battle Group involved in operations in and around Basra City.

After this tour of duty Steve was to be posted to a new job with promotion to Sergeant. Unfortunately this was not to be, as he was the victim of sniper fire whilst manning his tank, an FV510 Warrior, in the Mustashfa district in Basra.

Steve is buried in Dushorn Cemetery, Walsrode, Germany.

The Medals of Stephen Edwards

General Service Medal
Awarded for service in Northern Ireland.
Composition: Silver
Obverse: A crowned effigy of Queen Elizabeth II
Reverse: An oak wreath surrounding the words "For Campaign Service" surmounted by a crown
Ribbon: Purple with narrow green edge stripes
Clasp: Northern Ireland

The GSM was instituted in 1962 for personnel of all services for operations and campaigns that were not quite full-scale wars. Since the inception, thirteen campaigns have merited the award of a "clasp" in recognition. These are: Borneo, Radfan, South Arabia, Malay Peninsula, South Vietnam, Northern Ireland, Dhofar, Lebanon, Mine Clearance Gulf of Suez, Gulf, Kuwait, N. Iraq & S. Turkey and Air Operations Iraq.

The award of new clasps to the GSM discontinued on December 31 1999 as the Operational Service Medal was introduced on January 1 2000.

United Nations Medal for Cyprus
Awarded to the United Nations Peacekeeping Mission Force in Cyprus.
Composition: Bronze
Obverse: A central globe of the world surrounded by an olive leaf wreath with the capital letters "UN" above the globe
Reverse: Centrally the words "IN THE SERVICE OF PEACE"
Ribbon: UN blue with a central white stripe of equal width which is separated by two thin dark blue stripes

North Atlantic Treaty Organisation Medal
Awarded for service with NATO's KFOR in Kosovo.
Composition: Bronze
Obverse: The NATO Star emblem in a wreath of olive leaves
Reverse: The words "NORTH ATLANTIC TREATY ORGANISATION" around the edge and "IN SERVICE OF PEACE AND FREEDOM" in the centre, both of which are repeated in French
Ribbon: Blue with a central white stripe and thin white edges
Clasp: KOSOVO

The Iraq Medal
Awarded for service on Operation TELIC in Kuwait or Iraq in 2003.
Composition: Cupro-nickel
Obverse: A crowned effigy of Queen Elizabeth II
Reverse: The image of the Lamassu (a sculpture from the Assyrian period), above the word "IRAQ"
Ribbon: Sand coloured with central equally sized narrow stripes of black, white and red, representing the Iraqi flag
Clasp: "19 Mar to 28Apr 2003" awarded with the medal for service during the initial conflict in specified areas

Subsequent tours of duty to Iraq are not recognised by award of bars or numerals.

The Queen's Golden Jubilee Medal
Awarded to personnel of the Regular, Reserve and Cadet forces who were in effective service on February 6 2002, who had completed five years reckonable service.
Composition: Cupro-nickel with a gilt finish
Obverse: A crowned effigy of Queen Elizabeth II
Reverse: A shield of the Royal Coat of Arms surmounted by a crown and flanked by the dates "1952" and "2002"
Ribbon: Blue with narrow red edges. A central white stripe bisected by a thin red stripe

An FV510 Warrior tracked armoured vehicle.

World War 1 Rolls of Honour

Roll of Honour in St James' Church and carved on the Chancel panelling

Abbott	Arthur Randolphus	October 17 1918
Barratt	Ernest Wilfred	February 25 1919
Cobley	James Edward	October 21 1917
Cooper	William Edward	March 26 1915
Dingley	Horace	August 8 1916
Emery	Basil Frederick	February 17 1915
Ferrar	Septimus Leslie	April 9 1918
Giddings	John Thomas	May 9 1915
Gilbert	Herbert Frederick	April 21 1915
Guest	John William	October 7 1917
Hall	Hugh David	September 10 1916
Hiam	Robert Lewis	August 22 1918
Jeffery	Arthur William	November 2 1917
Johnson	George	March 21 1918
Loakes	Charles	December 4 1918
Loaring	William James	August 4 1917
Loveday	Alfred Shrives	March 21 1918
Makin	Philip	November 3 1914
Mayes	Ernest Harry	April 29 1918
Miller	Herbert	October 23 1916
Miller	Walter	November 3 1914
Morley	Joseph George	February 17 1917
Newman	Frederick William	October 8 1917
Newman	Sidney	October 1 1918
Nicholls	George Ernest	August 10 1916
Pollard	John Robert	July 7 1916
Raworth	Edward Percy	September 20 1917
Reeve	Horace William	May 28 1918
Reeve	William	March 26 1915
Richardson	Charles Edward	October 5 1915
Rogers	John	October 13 1918
Shadbolt	John Harry	January 7 1919
Simpson	George Henry	October 13 1915
Smith	George William Kenneth	October 22 1918
Smith	John Samuel	July 29 1916
Stimpson	John Thomas	August 25 1918
Sutcliffe	John Isaac Ashton	June 5 1916
Tarrant	Arthur	August 20 1918
Templeman	Richard Edis	May 9 1915

Throssell	Leonard	August 16 1917
Turner	George William	October 9 1916
Waite	Albert John	September 25 1915
Waite	Alfred Edward	March 14 1915
Wright	Samuel	September 24 1918

Total 44

Additional Names on the St James' Roll of Honour but not carved on the Chancel panelling

Arnold	George Edward	August 24 1916
Booth	Jonathan	October 30 1918
Holley	Percy John	August 27 1916
Wright	Arthur William	December 4 1918

Total 4

Additional Name on the Thrapston Baptist Church Roll of Honour but not carved on the Chancel panelling

Angood	Frederick Bowman	July 23 1918

Total 1

Additional Names on the Smith & Grace Roll of Honour but not carved on the Chancel panelling

Buckby	Ralph	September 26 1918
Langley	George Alfred	October 25 1916

Total 2

Additional Names on the Commonwealth War Graves Commission Site but not carved on the Chancel panelling or named on any Roll of Honour

Barrick	Thomas	June 6 1918
Earle	George Samuel	May 9 1915
Emery	Alexander John	March 7 1916
Johnson	Frederick William	January 5 1921
Lenton	Gerald	July 27 1917
Unger	George Abery	January 7 1916
Warren	Arthur Edward	June 1 1916

Total 7

Total 58

World War 2 and Iraq Rolls of Honour

World War 2

Roll of Honour in St James' Church and carved on the Chancel panelling

Barber	Leslie Ernest	February 6 1946
Bowyer	Thomas James	January 11 1943
Capps	William Charles Frank	May 1 1941
Cornwell	Jack	June 8 1940
Cullum	Aubrey Ernest	July 18 1943
Groom	Harold	June 11 1944
Hill	John William	October 30 1943
Hodson	Alfred Ernest	June 6 1943
Jackson	Christopher	December 27 1941
Smith	Robert Thomas	September 9 1943
Taney	Alfred William	November 7 1942

Total 11

Additional Name on the Commonwealth War Graves Commission Site but not carved on the Chancel panelling or on any Roll of Honour

Barber	Donald Francis	February 6 1945
Gifford	Frank Arthur	February 17 1945
Wagstaff	Herbert Brown	June 25 1944

Total 3

Total 14

Iraq War

Name carved on the Chancel panelling in St James' Church

Edwards	Stephen James	July 31 2007

Total 1

Other Thrapston Rolls of Honour

Thrapston Baptist Church

The plaque at the Baptist Church, Huntingdon Road, pictured below, contains the following inscriptions:

GREAT EUROPEAN WAR
ROLL OF HONOUR

Sig. Arthur R. Abbott	Age 19
Pte. Fred B. Angood	Age 35
Pte. Horace Dingley	Age 27
Pte. John W. Guest	Age 19
Pte. William J. Loaring	Age 29
Gnr. Ernest H. Mayes	Age 25
Pte. Fred W. Newman	Age 36
Pte. Sydney Newman	Age 21
Pte. John Robert Pollard	Age 26
Rflmn. Edward Percy Raworth	Age 22
Lieut. Kenneth Smith, R.A.F.	Age 19
Gnr. John H. Shadbolt	Age 20

"THEY GAVE THEIR ALL"

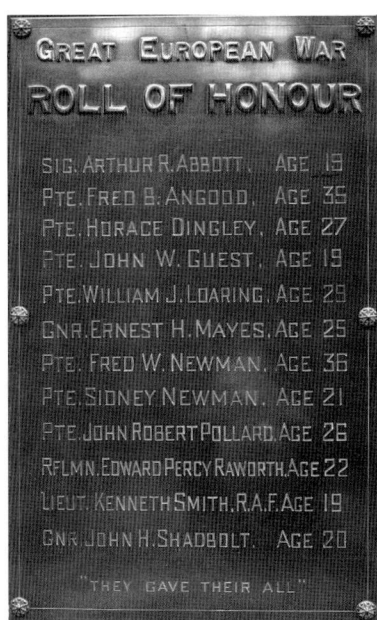

Smith and Grace Roll of Honour

The illuminated Roll of Honour is now displayed at the Thrapston Town Council Office, High Street.

ROLL OF HONOUR
FOR KING AND COUNTRY

The Following Employees of Smith & Grace Screw Boss Pulley Co. Ltd. have Joined H.M. Forces since the commencement of the Great War.

W	Charlton P.G.	Sergeant	1st Batt: Northants Regiment
W	Whiteman F.	Private	1st Batt: Northants Regiment
	Smith W.	Private	5th Batt: Northants Regiment
K	Reeve W.	Private	2nd Batt: Northants Regiment
K	Langley G. A.	Private	2nd Batt: Northants Regiment
W	George H.	Private	2nd Batt: Northants Regiment
	Swann A.G.	Private	A.S.C.
	Knight H.	Private	7th Batt: Northants Regiment
K	Giddings S. T.	Private	2nd Batt: Northants Regiment
K	Pollard J.	Private	2nd Batt: Northants Regiment
W	Thurlow T.	Private	2nd Batt: Northants Regiment
K	Buckby R.	2nd Lieut	R.A.F.
	Rogers S.	Private	3rd Batt: Northants Regiment
	Arnold G.	Private	4th Batt: Northants Regiment
	Cresswell T. B.	Private	R.A.M.C.
	March K. E.	Driver	R.F.A.
	Dingley T.	Gunner	R.F.A.
	Templeman T.	Private	A.S.C.(M.T.)
	Cooper E.	Private	R.A.M.C.
	Stobie W.	A.B.	Royal Navy
	Manning T. J.	Private	R.E.
W	Leete A.	Gunner	R.F.A.
	Thurlow H.	Private	M.G.C.
	Wills A.	Bandsman	2nd Batt: Beds Regiment
	Gunn H.	Private	2nd Batt: Northants Regiment
K	Loveday A. S.	Private	8th Batt: Royal West Surreys (Queen's)
	Frost T.	Private	4th Batt: East Surreys
	Manning J. T.	Driver	R.F.A.
	Guest H.	Private	A.S.C.(M.T.)
	Newman L.	Private	1/5 Batt: Royal West Surreys (Queen's)
	Pettit C.	Private	3rd Batt: East Kents (Buffs)
	Davis W.	Private	A.O.C.
W	Ireson W.	Private	4th Batt: Sherwood Foresters

Makin L. F.	Private	3rd Batt: Leicesters
Walker W. H.	Private	1/4 Batt: Northants Regiment
Cooper C. S.	Private	1/4 Batt: Northants Regiment
Edwards G.	Private	1/4 Batt: Northants Regiment

K. KILLED   **W.** WOUNDED

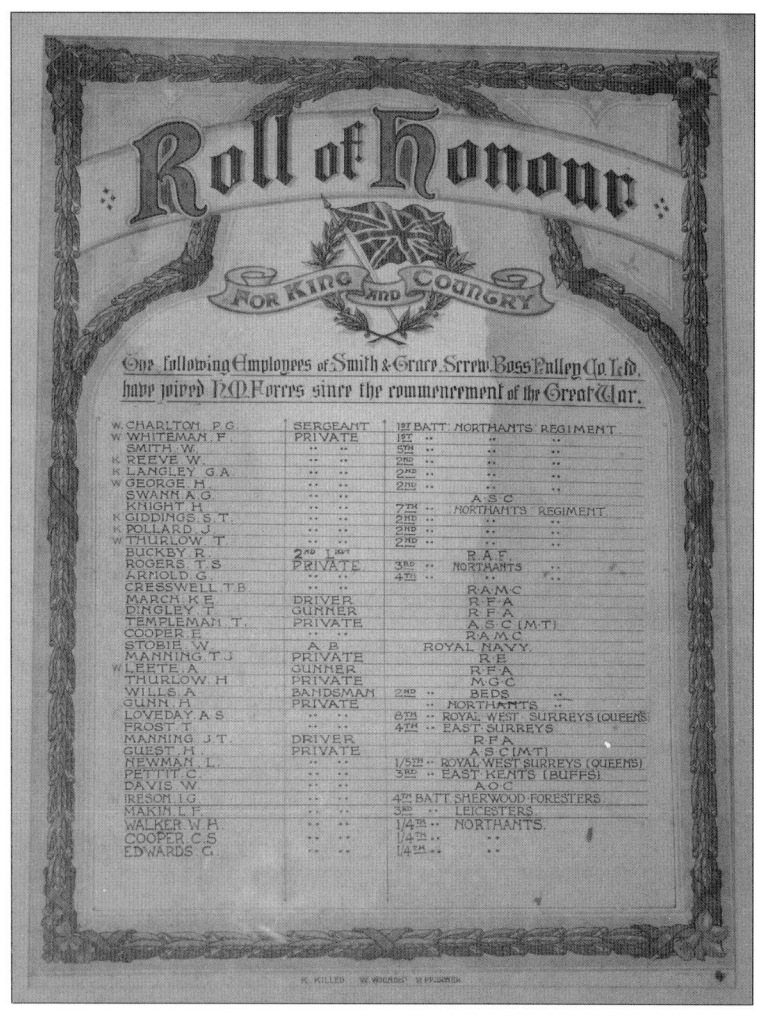

Thrapston Institute

(Northamptonshire Evening Telegraph – Wednesday January 26 1916)
        R. Templeman (who had given his life for his country)
        H. Nicholls
        W. Barber
        J. Barber
        W. Guest
        L. Farrer
        L. Abbott
        C. Read
        W. Clayson
        D. Skelton
        K. March
        H. Morris
        S. George
        W. George
        J. Nickerson
        P. Charlton
        M. G. W. Hunneybun
        E. March
        E. Mayes
        F. Holly
        J. G. Cresswell
        H. Guest
        N. Cotton
(L. Farrer and E. Mayes also subsequently died during the war.)
(L. Farrer is Septimus Leslie Ferrar – the above is how it was reported)

(Northamptonshire Evening Telegraph – Tuesday October 31 1916)
A meeting of the Games Committee was held at the Institute on Saturday evening, when Mr. J. W. Stubbs was unanimously elected games secretary until the end of the year, in place of Mr. J. C. Lavender, who has joined the colours. The number of members of the Institute now serving is 32.

Thrapston and District Rifle Shooting Club

(Northamptonshire Evening Telegraph – Friday January 25 1918)
The Chairman, in speaking of the work of the club, said that they had forty-one names on their Roll of Honour.

The whereabouts of these Rolls of Honour is unknown.

Remembrance, War Memorials and Peace Celebrations

On Wednesday February 17 1915, Thrapston Parish Council were requested by the County Council to forward a list of all those from the town who had enlisted or were serving in the war as soldiers or sailors, so that a complete record could be kept. The difficulty was that not all Thrapston men had joined up in the town. It was suggested that the town could be canvassed for names. The Town Clerk, Arthur G. Brown was asked to take the matter in hand. By the next meeting, Mr. Brown had divided the town into districts and produced a book for each. The councillors each were given a district and book. At the monthly meeting in September, it was announced that names had been collected and it was agreed to produce 20 copies of the full list to be posted in conspicuous places around town. It contained 203 names. It was accepted that it would require regular updates as a number of young men had joined up since the list was compiled. The town's population was given as 1,836, meaning that 11% of inhabitants had enlisted. The Rector, Rev. B. W. Stothert, proposed a permanent record be placed in the Parish Church when complete.

The Parish Church was not the only institution to have a Roll of Honour. In January 1916, the Thrapston Institute announced the names on its Roll of Honour (page 103). By October, 32 members of the Institute were serving.

By the summer of 1917, a rough draft of the Roll of Honour was placed in St. James' Church. Production of the Roll in book form was held in abeyance, partly because of the high price of vellum, but also that a definitive list could be produced thus negating the need for alterations or unnecessary spaces for additions.

In January 1918, the Thrapston and District Rifle Shooting Club announced that they had 41 names on their Roll of Honour.

By the end of the war, the Parish Church agreed that a Memorial in St. James' Church would be a fitting tribute to those who had become casualties of war. At the time, 42 parishioners had been killed, 2 were listed as "missing" and 227 men were either still serving or had been discharged. After discussion, it was agreed to approach Sir Thomas Graham Jackson, Bart, R.A., who had already designed work for the church, to produce plans for a permanent memorial to the dead. He accepted the commission and submitted drawings of the reredos, two figure panels and oak panelling, which were subsequently installed. The carving was done by Messrs. Thompson and Sons of Peterborough, the figure panels by Messrs. Farmer and Brindley of Peterborough and the panels and their inscription by Messrs. Pettit and Son from Thrapston.

A Service of Dedication to the Memorial to the Fallen was held at St. James' Church on Friday January 30 1920 at 7.30pm. The Dedication was made by the Venerable the Archdeacon of Oakham.

Original Drawing of the Reredos.

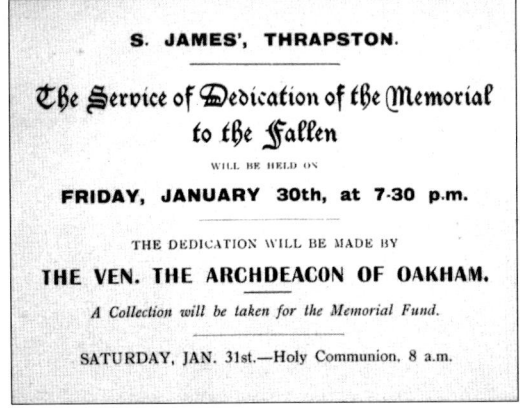

Invitation to the Dedication.

Detail of the central panel.

In January 1919, the Parish Council discussed having a town Memorial of the Peace and a committee comprising the Rector, Rev. H. E. Fitzherbert and Messrs. H. H. Bletsoe, J. T. Carress and A. French was appointed. By May, they had a number of suggestions and it was agreed to call a town meeting to discuss them. This occurred on Monday June 2 1919 at the Temperance Hall.

In total, seven suggestions were made by the meeting.
> That the Parish Church Memorial may be considered sufficient.
> A Recreation Ground be provided for the "rising generation".
> That the Temperance Hall be renovated as a public hall.
> The erection of an Isolation Hospital.
> The erection of a Market Cross.
> That, given the lack of baths in most homes, a Public Bath be provided.
> Playing fields be provided for football and cricket.

Each suggestion had supporters. The meeting eventually decided that a Recreation Ground was the preferred option and the inevitable committee (of 17 people) was appointed to progress the plan.

At the same meeting, it was agreed to hold Peace celebrations in town. This time, the committee comprised 24 people! The celebrations occurred between Saturday July 19 and Monday 21 July 1919. They were extensively publicised in the Northamptonshire Evening Telegraph on Wednesday 23 July 1919 and pictures of the Celebrations were published in the Thrapston and Raunds Journal on Friday 25 July 1919. Unfortunately, we have been unable to find a copy of the Journal.

The Saturday morning started early with a peal on the Church bells at twenty minutes to six, followed by a celebration of the Holy Communion at 7.30, 83 people attending. The Evening Telegraph reported *"At nine o'clock the children assembled at the council schools and were joined by members of the Parish Council and others. Mr. F. A. Cheney (chairman of the Parish Council) made an appropriate speech, in which he thanked all the workers for what they had done to make the day a success. He then hoisted the school flag and the Town Band played the National Anthem. The assembly then marched to the Rectory, and, headed by the band, continued in procession to the Market Hill, the band playing and the children singing "Onward Christian Soldiers.""*. A short service then ensued. The town had been decorated with flags and streamers across the roads and shops, hotels and houses also made great efforts. At midday, Market Hill was packed with spectators to watch the judging of the entrants in the fancy dress parade. This took about an hour. At about one o'clock *"a procession was formed in the following order: - The Town Crier, in his smart historical uniform; Mr. A. Bargh (one of the oldest inhabitants); Mr. R. Sanderson, and Special Constables Partridge and Sharpe; the Town Silver Band; demobilised soldiers and sailors (mostly in uniform); members of the Parish Council; the fancy dress characters; "Bright and Breezy" Band; and the decorated tradesmen's vehicles including two motor cars. The whole presented a very fascinating pageant, and took the usual route to the field adjoining "The Shrubberies" (kindly lent by Mrs. Sanderson), where some capital sports were provided for the children, cash prizes being given"*. Just before the sports, prizes were given for the fancy dress winners. The children's sports started at 2.00pm and lasted for two hours.

Food was provided for some of the population. *"At four o'clock an excellent free tea was provided in the Corn Exchange for children over three and under 15 years, 300 sitting down. Mr. W. Askew, C.C., attended the opening, and in a few appropriate words invited then to make a hearty meal of the good things provided.*
A very tempting meat tea was provided at the Co-operative Hall at five o'clock for the sailors and soldiers, when 130 sat down. The Rev. H. E. Fitzherbert, R.D., opened with a short speech. At the close Messrs. G. H. Gilbert and J. Webster expressed thanks on behalf of those present.
Simultaneously at five o'clock, at the Temperance Hall, the widows and wives of absent sailors and soldiers, and persons over 60 years, were entertained to a similar meat tea, 160 sitting down. The Rev. Mr. Gillians (Wesleyan minister) gave a short address of welcome".

During the evening, sports were held for adults whilst the Silver Band played, both during the sports and afterwards for dancing.

On Sunday July 20, a Church service to celebrate the Peace was held in St. James' Church.

The next day, Monday July 21, the inmates of the Thrapston Poor Law Institution *"...held their Peace celebration dinner on Monday instead of Saturday. The three local Guardians, Mrs. G. Smith, the Rev. H. E. Fitzherbert, R.D., and Mr. T. S. Agutter, J.P., were present and assisted in the serving of the tempting fare provided.*
After the dinner the master, Mr. H. Elks, proposed a vote of thanks to the Guardians, to which all three Guardians replied. Tobacco and beer were served to the men; tea, sugar, and biscuits to the women; and wine to the infirmary patients.
During the evening the old people were entertained by Mr. Horace Wilton, who gave several character sketches, and kept his audience thoroughly amused for about two hours. A gramophone, kindly lent by Mr. F. Apethorpe, added greatly to the inmates' enjoyment, and was highly appreciated".

In April 1920, the announcement was made that agreement had been reached with Major Buckley to purchase the field opposite Thrapston House. The money was paid over by the Parish Council on September 29 1920. The cost was £700 for the 2.5 acre site. After some debate, it was agreed that the Parish Council should accept the trusteeship of the Recreation Ground. It was named The Peace Memorial Park and remains to this day.

World War 1 Campaign Medals and Bronze Plaque

The 1914 Star, made of bronze, was awarded to all personnel who *"served with the establishment of their unit in France and Belgium between the 5th August and midnight on the 22nd/23rd November 1914"*.

The 1914/1915 Star, also made of bronze, was awarded to all who had *"served in a theatre of war, anywhere in the world, before the 31st December 1915 but who did not qualify for the 1914 Star"*.

The British War Medal, made of silver, was awarded to a member of the fighting forces who *"had to leave the shores of their country in any part of the British Empire whilst on active service"*.

The Victory Medal, made of bronze, was awarded to *"all who entered a theatre of war"*.

The Bronze Memorial Plaque, commonly known as the "Death Plaque" or "Death Penny", was designed by Edward Carter-Preston and given to the next of kin of anyone who lost their life on active service during the Great War. Each was personalised with the casualty's name. The official figure for the number of plaques issued is over 1,360,000 plaques from early 1919 until the 1930's. In reality, there was a significantly higher number made. The first Memorial Plaque Factory was at Church Road, Acton, London W3 and produced plaques from 1919 until December 1920, when production was transferred to the Royal Arsenal at Woolwich. The Woolwich plaques all have a combined "WA" mark on the back. Very occasionally, an error appeared as in the case of James Morris McNESS of the Royal Field Artillery (not a local man) whose plaque recorded his surname as McMESS.

Of the local casualties, we are grateful to relatives for allowing us to photograph bronze plaques in their possession, pictures of which appear on the next page.

All were cast at Woolwich and are quite early. The first "H" in "HE DIED FOR FREEDOM AND HONOUR" is described as Wide. Later plaques had narrower "H's", designed so that when an occasional female casualty needed commemorating, the "S" could be easily inserted into the mould, thus reading "SHE". Each plaque had a number between the lion's rear leg and tail. These probably identified the work of an individual bronze caster. The Thrapston plaques carry numbers 25 (Alfred Waite) and 84 (James Loaring). All "SHE DIED" plaques carry the number 11.

Two plaques to local men are shown below.

Alfred Edward Waite.

William James Loaring.

World War 2 Stars and Medals

The 1939 – 45 Star can be considered to be the qualifying one, as those entitled to it became entitled to the others on entering the particular theatres of operations, except in the case of the Atlantic, Air Crew Europe and Africa Stars. No one person could receive more than five of the stars and the two medals as seen below:

1939 – 45 Star
Atlantic Star (or France and Germany Star, or Air Crew Europe Star)
Africa Star
Pacific Star (or Burma Star)
Italy Star
Defence Medal
War Medal

All of the eight stars are of the same design, the only difference being the wording around the central circle.

Composition:	Bronze
Size:	1.75in. across
Obverse:	Six pointed star. In the centre the Royal Cipher surmounted by a crown, with a surrounding circle bearing the title.
Reverse:	Plain
Ribbons:	All 1.25in. wide. Varying with each star and passing through a suspension ring attached to the topmost point of the star. The designs were by H.M. King George VI.
Naming:	All issued unnamed by the British Government

The 1939 – 45 Star

Awarded for service between September 3 1939 and September 2 1945.
Service which was ended by death, or disability due to service, would qualify for the award, even if the qualifying period had not been reached.
The colours of the ribbon are, from the left, dark blue, red and light blue in equal proportion, to symbolize the Royal and Merchant Navies, the Army and the Royal Air Force.

The Atlantic Star

For service between September 3 1939 and May 8 1945.
Awarded to commemorate the Battle of the Atlantic.
The ribbon is of the watered type from the left, dark blue, white and sea green representing the Atlantic

The Air Crew Europe Star
Awarded for service between September 3 1939 and June 5 1944.
To those flying operationally from UK bases over Europe.
The ribbon is light blue with black edges and two yellow stripes, symbolizing continuous service both night and day.

The Africa Star
For service in North Africa between June 10 1940 and May 12 1943.
The ribbon is pale buff with a central red stripe and two narrow stripes, one dark blue, to the left and the other light blue, representing the desert, the Royal and Merchant Navies, the Army and the Royal Air Force.

The Pacific Star
For service in the Pacific theatre of operations between December 8 1941 and September 2 1945.
The ribbon is dark green with red edges. There is a central yellow stripe with a thin dark blue stripe to the left and another light blue to the right. The green and yellow symbolize the forests and beaches, the dark blue the Royal and Merchant Navies, the red the Army and the light blue the Royal Air Force.

The Burma Star
This star was awarded for service between December 11 1941 and September 2 1945.
The ribbon is dark blue with a wide red stripe down the centre, with a thin orange stripe on either side. The red representing the British Commonwealth Forces and the orange the sun.

The Italy Star
Awarded for service between June 11 1943 and May 8 1945.
To those involved in operations in Sicily or Italy.
The ribbon has red, white, green, white and red stripes of equal width that represent the colours of Italy.

The France and Germany Star
This star was awarded for service in operations between June 6 1944 and May 8 1945 in France, Belgium, Holland or Germany, from D-Day to the German surrender.
The ribbon has equal width stripes of blue, white, red, white and blue, symbolic of the Union Flag and those of France and the Netherlands. It will be noted that the colours of Belgium are not represented.

The Defence Medal
This was awarded for service between September 3 1939 and September 2 1945.

Composition:	Cupro-nickel
Size:	1.42in. diameter
Obverse:	An uncrowned head of King George VI with the legend GEORGIVS VI D : G : BR : OMN : REX F : D : IND : IMP :
Reverse:	An oak tree with the Royal crown above, flanked on each side by lions counter rampant. The dates 1939 and 1945 are on either side with the title THE DEFENCE MEDAL at the bottom.
Ribbon:	Flame coloured with green edges with a thin black stripe down the centre of the green stripes. Representing the enemy attacks on our green land. The black-out is commemorated by the black stripes.
Naming:	Issued unnamed.

The War Medal
Awarded for service between September 3 1939 and September 2 1945.

For all full-time personnel of the Armed Forces wherever their war service was carried out. Operational and non-operational service counted, providing that it was of at least twenty-eight days duration.

Composition:	Cupro-nickel
Size:	1.42in. diameter
Obverse:	The crowned head of the King surrounded by the legend GEORGIVS VI D : G : BR : OMN : REX ET INDIAE IMP :
Reverse:	A lion standing on a fallen dragon, with the dates 1939 and 1945 at the top.
Ribbon:	Stripes of red, blue, white, blue and red, with a thin red stripe centrally down the white stripe. The colours of the Union Flag.
Naming:	Issued unnamed.

As with the Stars, the Medals had various qualifying conditions too numerous to go into here.

The German White Flag Treachery

On September 17 1914, during the battle of the Aisne, members of the German 53rd Regiment were firing from behind a ridge. Unexpectedly, a white flag appeared from their lines and this led the Northampton's to believe that the enemy were ready to surrender. A Company of the 1st Battalion Northamptonshire Regiment left their trench at the foot of the slope and advanced towards the enemy, who pretended not to understand that they were to place their rifles on the ground and hold up their hands. A few Germans laid down their rifles, at which the men in front fell flat on the ground and a second line, which had been concealed behind the ridge, appeared and fired at the Northampton's. Unprepared for such an assault, they were mercilessly cut down. Unluckily for the enemy, flanking them and only some 400 yards away, was a machine gun manned by a detachment of the 1st Queen's Royal West Surrey Regiment. They at once opened fire, cutting a lane through the Germans, who retreated to their own trench with great loss. Shortly afterward they were driven further back, with additional loss, by a battalion of Guards which came up in support.

A number of similar instances were recorded during the early days of the war. They were reported in the newspapers and shortly after, the war artist Fortunino Matania, an Italian, published a drawing depicting the scene in the weekly publication "The Sphere" entitled "The abuse of the white flag", shown below. He worked and lived with the men in the trenches and was able to produce pictures which appealed to the demand back home for heroic deeds.

Approximately 100 members of the 1st Battalion went forward that day. Only eight escaped with their lives, including Privates Philip Makin (page 3) and Walter Miller (page 4).

Having survived September 17, the two Thrapston soldiers only lived a further 46 days, both being wounded on November 2 and dying the next day.

The Thrapston Chums

During World War 1 there was an ever-increasing need for volunteers. The famous Lord Kitchener poster "Your country needs you" was not enough to bring forward the necessary numbers, so General Henry Rawlinson suggested to Government that they recruit through Pals, Chums or Local battalions. Men would enlist with their friends, train and then serve at the front with them. Larger communities soon had Pals battalions – Birmingham, Sheffield, Leeds and Accrington to name a few. Whilst this was good news for the military, it soon resulted in communities losing large numbers of men, often in the course of one action and after the Somme in 1916, the practice stopped.

Thrapston was never going to be able to provide sufficient men to form a battalion. Kelly's Directory of Northamptonshire for 1914 gives the town's population as 1,836 whilst a total of 285 men are named on the Roll of Honour, a very significant proportion.

On Friday July 21 1916, the Kettering Leader carried a grainy picture and story about "Sporting Thrapston Boys", subtitled "Another Chum Dies a Soldier's Death". This referred to John Pollard (page 25).

Twenty men are pictured, with their dogs, and named. Of these, six joined the Northamptonshire Regiment, half of them being killed – John Pollard, George Nicholls and Walter Miller. Of the others, Samuel Wright and Jonathan Booth also did not survive the war. Of the remaining 15 men, many received wounds of varying degrees.

Another picture of Thrapston Argyll Football Club taken in the 1909 – 1910 season shows eleven players with their manager and trainer. Three players have been identified – John Pollard standing centrally in the back row wearing the goalkeeper's shirt, John Giddings on the left of the middle row and Richard Templeman at the right in the front row. It is almost certain that the others enlisted as well. John Giddings and Richard Templeman were killed on the same day in 1915, John near Armentieres and Richard during the battle of Aubers Ridge. This battle was one of the bloodiest during the war, there being about 11,000 casualties on May 9, most within yards of their own trenches. As well as Richard, George Earl also died as did six men from Raunds and Stanwick.

Today it is difficult to comprehend the effect on local communities at having so many of their young men killed. Days such as May 9 1915, where Thrapston lost three were, mercifully, scarce. Of those who survived that day's carnage, Fairey Whiteman had a hand blown off. He returned to Halford Street on September 8 1915, having been fitted with an artificial hand, to find the entire street decorated with flags and bunting.

The Loss of HMS Glorious 1940

From June 5 to June 8 1940, Operation Alphabet was underway. This was the evacuation of all British and Allied Forces from Norway. Two troop convoys were formed and the first sailed on June 7 and the second on June 8. Both convoys safely reached the U.K.

Aircraft carriers, HMS Ark Royal and HMS Glorious were operating together and Glorious had flown on 20 RAF fighters to return to Britain, also on board were 10 fighters and 5 torpedo bombers of Fleet Air Arm. Together they were to have made up part of the escort of the second convoy.

During the early hours of Saturday June 8, Glorious signalled the Vice Admiral on Ark Royal for permission to proceed independently to Scapa Flow. This request was approved and Glorious and her two destroyer escort, HMS Ardent and HMS Acasta, set off on a zig-zag course to confuse enemy submarines.

By 4.00pm Glorious was moving at about 17 knots, with the destroyers about 440 metres off either bow. None of the three ships had radar and no aircraft was sent up for observation. No lookout was posted to the crow's nest of Glorious.
The sea was calm with good visibility. Wind force was 2-3 and the sea temperature was 1 degree Centigrade.

Just after 4.00pm two ships were sighted on the western horizon and Ardent was sent off to investigate and identify them. Action Stations was sounded at 4.20pm.

They had been intercepted by the German Battlecruisers Scharnhorst and Gneisenau. At 4.30pm, when at a range of about 16 miles they opened fire. Ardent had closed and was fired on by Gneisenau. She withdrew, firing guns and torpedoes at the Germans.

Glorious had been hit heavily at 4.38pm and the destroyers made smoke to screen her from further attack. This was effective for around half an hour. Ardent had received many hits and sank about 5.25pm.

The smoke screen had been worked, but as it cleared Glorious was struck many times again. The bridge had been hit killing the Captain and most of the bridge personnel. The Germans ceased fire at 5.40pm and Glorious sank about 6.10pm.

Acasta had fired torpedoes at the Scharnhorst, one of which hit, causing damage and casualties. Turning away Acasta was caught by heavy accurate fire and at 6.20pm she sank.

From these three British vessels 1531 men lost their lives. Only 38 men were to survive the action. Marine Jack Cornwell (page 77) was one of those lost.

The Scharnhorst firing at the Glorious, June 8 1940.

Acasta   Glorious   Ardent

The Battle for Primasole Bridge
July 1943

Primasole Bridge from the south.

After the invasion of Sicily by the Allies on July 10 1943, it was important to push on towards Messina without delay. From the British landings at Avola the advance onto the Plain of Catania required the capture of the Primasole and Malati bridges before the retreating Axis forces could destroy them.

Fierce fighting took place between German and British airborne troops, which had reached Primasole Bridge with about 200 men and three anti-tank guns. They had seized the bridge and removed the demolition charges, set up a perimeter defence and being heavily attacked they had to withdraw to some high ground overlooking the bridge from where they were able to prevent the Germans from destroying it.

Progress was very slow and there was only one road to Primasole Bridge, which was mined and had vehicles blocking the road, an attack on July 15 failed, as the tanks of 44th Royal Tank Regiment could not cross the bridge.

Before dawn on July 16 a further attack was made by the 8th Battalion, Durham Light Infantry and a bridgehead was secured just large enough to let sappers clear the mines and obstructions. This was done in time to allow a squadron of 44th RTR pass over the bridge. The bridgehead was under accurate anti tank fire and four tanks were lost.

On the night of July 16/17, the 6th and 9th Durhams put in further attacks to extend the bridgehead, which allowed the tanks of the Sharpshooters ($3^{rd}/4^{th}$ County of London Yeomanry, R.A.C.) to support this extension. During the battle to achieve this, the Sharpshooters were to lose their CO and five tank commanders through sniping. The bridge was now secured and the Sharpshooters were then relieved by tanks of 44th RTR on July 18 and during the day they had a fierce fight assisting the 1st Royal Berkshires, who had been surrounded by the Germans. Another five tanks were knocked out during this action. This was when Aubrey Cullum (page 83) was to lose his life.

On July 19, the 44th RTR supported an advance from the bridgehead, but little progress could be made due to the strong opposition and another five tanks were to be lost or severely damaged. Further attacks were made on July 20 and these proved to be successful, allowing the advance to Catania to continue.

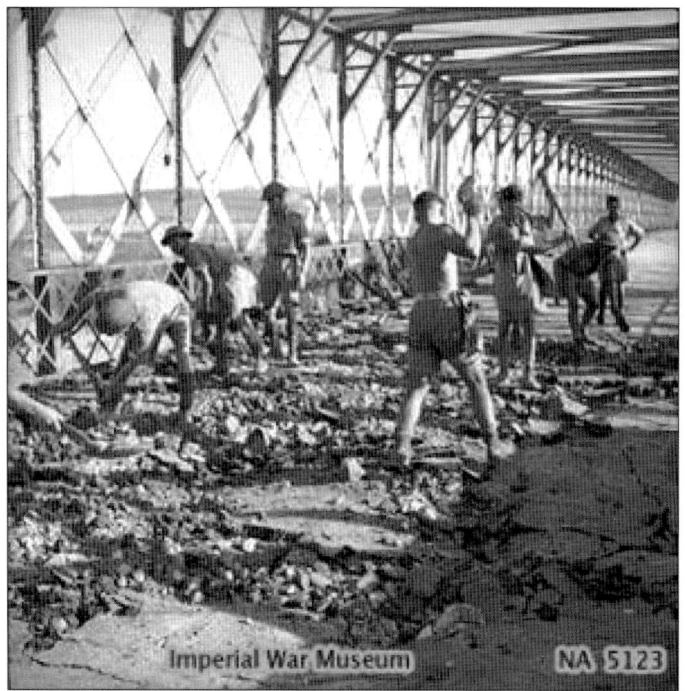

Sappers of the Royal Engineers repairing damage
to Primasole Bridge after its capture.

Let Not Those Kind F-words Be Lost

All lost?
The heroes dead?
Troy gate swings useless on its post
Where Hector in full sun
Fell, while his blood played and shone
Though Troy crack, seven wails burn,
Let not those words be lost
Which Paris, lacking Greek,
Fumbled into Helen's breast
While worlds grew warm.
Let not those kind F-words be lost
Of Aubrey Cullum at Primasole Bridge:
Of my friend Hugh Bishop on the Sangro
Delicately shrapnel-wounded in the tank, soon dead.
Ken Sinden, serious drinker, young Robin Anderson
The Scot, companions brewing merrily in petrol engined
Sherman tank, in Normandy, July, Hill One-One-Two.
Jack Thorogood at St Oedenrode; Len Williams
Joking, wounded, pipe in hand, with Benny Shaw.
"No word of theirs is lost," the padre hazarded.
"No lie unsaid," they laughing all replied.

By Denis Knight (44th Royal Tank Regiment R.A.C.)
Written in tribute to the 230 men of his regiment
that gave their lives in North Africa and Europe
1941 – 1945.

"Gallivanting Gunner" from Thrapston

From an article in the Thrapston, Raunds and Oundle Journal, August 13 1943.

"Gallivanting Gunner" from Thrapston.
"Bishops are a grand weapon" says Bombardier.

Below a Thrapston man tells about the capabilities of assault guns nicknamed "Bishops" which can go across the roughest country and don't have to wait for the REs (Royal Engineers) to put things right when a blown up road is encountered.

Battering the German and Italian forces from their strong points or the craggy heights of the hills to the west of Mount Etna have been the "Bishop Boys" – the gunners who man the self propelled assault guns.

Tagged "Bishops" by their crews the guns 25pdrs are mounted on Valentine tank chassis. An armour box which houses and protects the gun and crew has also earned the nickname "Cannon Caravans".

Up steep rocky hillsides, through bomb craters and demolitions left by the retreating Axis the Bishops have advanced. "They're just the job for this hilly country we've struck now" said Bombardier Robert Smith of Washington Street, Thrapston, commander of one of the Bishops. "They can go across the roughest country and up any hills. When Jerry blows up a road we don't have to wait for the Engineers to come up, we just go straight through. This armour is a great thing too. We had ordinary field guns before and believe me when small arms stuff is whistling about it is pretty chilly behind the shield of a field gun. Now though with these Bishops we can get anywhere and get into action right away. The 'Gallivanting Gunners' is a good name for us".

Perched on the back slope of a hill the Bishops looked like giant frogs waiting to leap (writes a military observer). A few minutes before they had advanced up a dusty country road to take up a new position. Straight off the road they swung onto the hillside. Behind them came the Command Post tank from which the troop leader directed the fire. Within two minutes the guns were lined up, fire orders came over the radio and shells were whistling their way towards the German positions. Occasionally when orders were received to switch targets and the limited traverse of the gun was not sufficient, the whole tank had to be swung. "But it's an easy job when you get used to it" said Driver Harry Lugg of St. Ives, Cornwall. "We got so used to the feel of the tank that we can swing them to within half a degree and it's great to be inside here when anything is flying about. Give me the old Bishop anytime rather than the ordinary gun tower".

"Bishop" QF 25pdr on Valentine carrier, Mk1.

Manufactured by Birmingham Railway Carriage and Wagon Company from 1941 – 42.
Weight 17.5 tons, length 5.53m, width 2.63m, height 2.83m.
Armour, hull 8 – 60mm, superstructure 13 – 51mm
Armament, QF 25pdr gun-howitzer with 32 rounds
Secondary armament, .303 Bren Machine Gun
Operational range, 145 km (90 miles)
Crew, four (commander, gunner, loader and driver)

A "Bishop" in action in Italy.

Plan of Oundle Road Cemetery, Thrapston

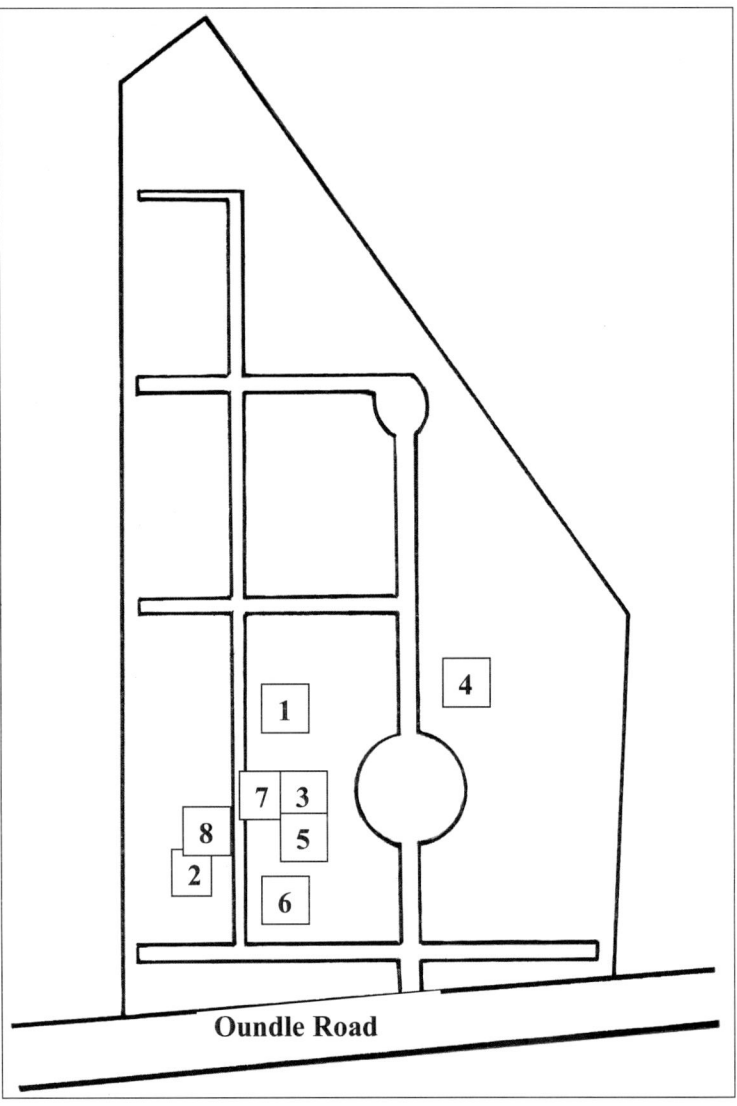

1. Charles Loakes (page 66)
2. John Thomas Stimpson (page 58)
3. Walter and Herbert Miller (pages 4 and 33)
4. Arthur Randolphus Abbott (page 63)
5. George and Frederick William Johnson (pages 49 and 73)
6. John Samuel Smith (page 26)
7. Frank Arthur Gifford (page 89)
8. William Charles Frank Capps (page 78)

Index

Abbeville, France 79
ABBOTT Arthur Randolphus 63, 97, 100, 124
Adnitt Bros., Northampton 22
Agny, France 38
Agutter T.S. (Justice of the Peace) 108
Aisne, Battle of 114
Albert, France 57
Aldwincle, Northamptonshire 12, 16
Alexandria, Egypt 71, 86
Amiens, France 52
ANGOOD Frederick Bowman 55, 98, 100
Annaba, Algeria 82
Apethorpe F. 108
Arabian Gulf 93
Arcade, Italy 65
Armentiers, France 13, 116
ARNOLD George Edward 29, 98
Arras, France 38, 49
Askew W. (County Councillor) 107
Asplen Daisy 89
Aubers Ridge, France 12, 14, 116
Authville Wood, Thiepval, France 37
Aveluy, France 28, 30
Avola, Sicily 83, 119

Bailey Margaret Mary 66
Bamford Joan 90
Banbury, Oxfordshire 53
BARBER Donald Francis 88, 99
BARBER Leslie Ernest 88, 90, 99
Barclays Bank 37
Bargh A. 107
Barnard Mr., bootmaker, Thrapston 59
Barnett M., coachbuilder, Thrapston 51, 57
BARRATT Ernest Wilfred 71, 72, 97
Barrack Row, Islip 45
BARRICK Thomas 54, 98
Basra, Iraq 93
Beeston, Nottinghamshire 31
Benyon Colonel 65
Berneville, France 29
Bethune, France 17
Beugny, France 62
Billow Wood, France 58
Bishop Self Propelled Gun 84, 122, 123
Bletsoe H.H. 106
Bletsoe's, Thrapston 81

Bois Grenier, France 15
Bombay, India 7, 63
Booth Annie 80
BOOTH Jonathan (Jack) 65, 98, 115
Boulogne, France 10
BOWYER Thomas James 81, 99
Brampton, Huntingdonshire 82
Bray-sur-Somme, France 57, 58
British and Empire Military Units
    Australian Clearing Station 3rd 64
    Army Service Corps 31, 39, 57, 60
    Badger Squadron 93
    Battery 'B', 98 Brigade 21
    Bedfordshire Regiment, 1st Battalion 11
    Brigades 17th 85
              35th 79
              98th 21
              111th 39
              286th 51
    Canadian General Hospital No.1 29
    Canadian Infantry 16th Battalion 40
    Canadian Mounted Rifles 1st 24
    Casualty Clearing Station 20th 72
                        57th 66
    Cheshire Regiment 88, 90
    Chindit Brigade 87
    Divisions 5th 85
              12th 79
              20th Indian 87
              37th 39
    Durham Light Infantry 54, 119
    East Surrey Regiment 27
    Field Ambulance 8th 49
    General Hospital No.9 BEF 33
                      No.11 BEF 10
    Gloucestershire Regiment 1/6th Battalion 67
    Grenadier Guards 1st Battalion 31
                    3rd Battalion 31, 50
    Hertfordshire Regiment 1/1st Battalion 30
    Honourable Artillery Company 38
    Hospital, 3rd Echelon, Egypt 71
    Huntingdonshire Cyclist Battalion 30, 42, 58
    Indian Tank Brigade 267th 81
    Irish Guards Battle Group 93
    King's Royal Rifle Corps 71
    Leicestershire Regiment 1st Battalion 59, 90
    London Regiment 22nd Battalion 57
    Machine Gun Corps 27, 32, 42, 43, 71
    Manitoba Regiment 40
    Middlesex Regiment 19th Battalion 55
    Northamptonshire Regiment 59, 60, 67

        1st Battalion 3, 4, 9, 12, 14, 26, 114
        2nd Battalion 8, 10, 12, 13, 15, 25, 34, 44, 85
        1/4th Battalion 16, 45, 56
        5th Battalion 17, 28, 29
        6th Battalion 37
        7th Battalion 22
        8th Battalion 13
Northamptonshire Yeomanry 1/1st Battalion 65
North Staffordshire Regiment 9th Battalion 72
Queen Alexandra Military Extension Hospital, London 26
Queen's Royal West Surrey Regiment 51, 57, 66
                1st Battalion 114
                7th Battalion 79
                8th Battalion 50
                10th Battalion 33
RSU (Repair Servicing Unit) 109, R.A.F. 82
Rifle Brigade 2nd Battalion 53
        11th Battalion 41
Royal Air Force 60
Royal Air Force Volunteer Reserve 82, 88
Royal Armoured Corps 163 Regiment 81
Royal Army Medical Corps 49, 60
Royal Army Pay Corps 89
Royal Army Service Corps 86
Royal Artillery, 55 AA/Anti Tank Regiment 87
        55 Light Anti Aircraft Regiment 87
            142 Field Regiment (Royal North Devon Yeomanry) 84
Royal Berkshire Regiment 1st Battalion 120
Royal Electrical and Mechanical Engineers 86
Royal Engineers 22, 44, 54, 72, 86, 120, 122
        94th Field Company 54
Royal Field Artillery 21, 51, 52, 62, 73
Royal Flying Corps 64
Royal Fusiliers 2/4th (City of London) Battalion 58
        13th Battalion 39
Royal Marine Light Infantry 23
Royal Marines 77
Royal Navy 63
Royal North Devon Yeomanry (142 Field Regiment R.A.) 84
Royal Sussex Regiment 32, 43
Royal Tank Regiment 2nd 93
        44th 83, 119, 121
Royal Warwickshire Regiment 1/8th Battalion 30
Sharpshooters, 3rd/4th County of London Yeomanry, R.A.C. 119
Sherwood Foresters (Notts and Derby Regiment) 13th Battalion 81
Squadron 99, R.A.F. 60
Tank Corps 44th Battalion 73
Topcliffe, R.A.F., Yorkshire 82
York and Lancaster Regiment 6th Battalion 61
Bronfay, France 58
Bronze Plaques (Death Penny) 109

Brow Head, Ireland 7
Brown Arthur G. (Thrapston Town Clerk) 104
BUCKBY Ralph 60, 98, 101
Buckden, Huntingdonshire 81, 82
Buckley Major 108
Burma 81
Burton Latimer, Northamptonshire 60, 78
Bythorn, Huntingdonshire 40, 44

Cambridge 8
Canada 24, 40, 88, 93
Canadian First World War Book of Remembrance 24
CAPPS William Charles Frank 78, 99, 124
Carress J.T. 106
Catania, Sicily 83, 119, 120
Catterick, Yorkshire 93
Caulincourt, France 59
Cemeteries and Memorials
    Adelaide Cemetery, France 52
    Arras Memorial, France 49
    Berlin 1939 – 1945 War Cemetery, Germany 79
    Bethune Town Cemetery, France 17
    Bone War Cemetery, Algeria 82
    Boulogne Eastern Cemetery, France 10
    Bray Military Cemetery, France 57
    Bronfay Farm Military Cemetery, France 58
    Burton Latimer War Memorial 60
    Cassino Memorial, Italy 84
    Cassino War Cemetery, Italy 85
    Catania War Cemetery, Sicily 83
    Charleroi Communal Cemetery, Belgium 72
    Deir El Belah War Cemetery, Israel 71
    Delsaux Farm Cemetery, France 62
    Dely Ibrahim War Cemetery, Algeria 90
    Denford War Memorial 29, 34
    Dueville Communal Cemetery Extension, Italy 67
    Dushorn Cemetery, Germany 93
    Etaples Military Cemetery, France 29
    Field Ambulance Cemetery No.7, Gallipoli 16
    Gaza War Cemetery, Israel 45
    Giavera British Cemetery, Italy 65
    Guards Cemetery, Cuinchy, France 9
    Imphal War Cemetery, Burma 87
    Kettering War Memorial 26
    Kviberg Cemetery, Sweden 23
    Lahana Military Cemetery, Greece 27
    Leeds (Lawns Wood) Cemetery 80
    Le Touret Memorial, France 8, 12, 14
    Lijssenthoek Military Cemetery, Belgium 38, 55
    Madras War Cemetery, India 81

Marfaux British Cemetery, France 54
Maroc British Cemetery, France 40
Menin Gate Memorial, Belgium 11, 24, 39
Menin Road South Military Cemetery, Belgium 22
Mikra British Cemetery, Greece 21
Motor Car Corner Cemetery, Belgium 44
Moulin-les Metz Commune Cemetery, France 60
Naples War Cemetery, Italy 86
Northamptonshire 1/4th Battalion Cemetery, Gallipoli 16
Oundle War Memorial 88
Ploegsteert Memorial, Belgium 13,15
Plymouth Naval Memorial 77
Poperinghe Old Military Cemetery, Belgium 4
Pozieres British Cemetery, France 28
Pozieres Memorial, France 50
Ramsey War Memorial 58
Rue David Military Cemetery, France 51
St Ruffine Commune Cemetery, France 60
St Sever Cemetery, France 33
Soissons Memorial, France 53
Terlincthun British Cemetery, France 64
Theipval Memorial, France 25, 30, 31, 32, 34, 37
Thrapston Cemetery 4, 26, 33, 49, 58, 63, 73, 89
Titchmarsh War Memorial 83
Trefcon British Cemetery, France 59
Trimulghery No.12 Military Cemetery, India 81
Tyne Cot Memorial, Belgium 41,42
Valenciennes (St Roch) Communal Cemetery, France 66
Vis-en-Artois Memorial, France 61
Welsh Cemetery (Caesar's Nose), Belgium 43
Ypres Town Cemetery Extension, Belgium 3

Central Council Memorial Book of Church Bell Ringers 62
Chatham, Kent 63
Cheney F.A. 107
Chester College 80
Christchurch, Hampshire 38
City Road, London 21
COBLEY James Edward 44, 97
Colchester, Essex 59
Coleman John , Flight Sergeant 88
Commonwealth War Graves Commission 26
Contalmaison, France 26
COOPER William Edward 9, 10, 97
CORNWELL Jack 77, 99, 118
Cranford, Northamptonshire 50
Croxton, Cambridgeshire 11
Cuinchy, France 9
CULLUM Aubrey Ernest 83, 99, 120, 121
Cyprus 93,94

Dardenelles 16
David Mr D.W., farmer, Thrapston 45
Davis M., fishmonger, Thrapston 43
De Havilland 9 60
Denford, Northamptonshire 23, 29, 34, 56
        Church Choir 23
        Cricket Club 86
        Football Club 56
        High Street 29, 56
        Lodge 12
Diamond Cyril 90
DINGLEY Horace 27, 97, 100
Ditchingham, Norfolk 21
Dresden, Germany 79
Dunkirk, France 85

Eaglehurst College, Northampton 64
EARLE George Samuel 10, 12, 14, 15, 98, 116
Earl's Barton, Northamptonshire 80
Earl's Groom, Worcestershire 31
EDWARDS Stephen James 93, 99
Egypt 45, 49, 56, 71, 86
Elks H. 108
EMERY Alexander John 22, 98
EMERY Basil Frederick 7, 97
Emery Frederick (Headmaster) 7, 21
Enfield, Middlesex 80
Epinoy, France 61
Estaires, France 51
Evening Telegraph 21, 22, 31, 78, 103, 106, 107

Farmer & Brindley, Peterborough 104
Fejja, Egypt 56
FERRAR Septimus Leslie 51, 97, 103
Fife Street, Northampton 22
Fitzherbert Rev. H.E. (Rector of Thrapston) 37, 82, 106, 107, 108
Flers, France 33
Fletton Mr.W., Thorpe Achurch 87
Fleurbaix, France 51
Foundry Yard, Glinton 17
Franks Florence M. 26
Freeman T., farmer, Denford 29
Freeman & Webb, builders, Thrapston 23
French A. 106
Fricourt Contalmaison, France 25

Garratt Phyllis May 82
Gallipoli 16

Gaza, Third Battle of 45
German 53rd Regiment 114
GIDDINGS John Thomas 13, 14, 25, 97, 101, 116
GIFFORD Frank Arthur 89. 99, 124
GILBERT Herbert Frederick 8, 11, 97
Gilbert Stanley, Lt. R.A.F. 60
Gillians Rev. Mr., Wesleyan minister, Thrapston 107
Glenn Mr., hairdresser, Thrapston 63
Glinton, Northamptonshire 17
Gosport, Hampshire 63
Great Addington, Northamptonshire 66
Great Staughton, Huntingdonshire 53
Green The, Islip 21
Grenay, France 40
Grimsby, Lincolnshire 37
Grensell, electrical contractors, Kettering 86
GROOM Harold 86, 99
GUEST John William 41, 42, 97, 100

Haddenham, Cambridgeshire 67
Halbard Peter 50
Hall Gertrude 44
HALL Hugh David 31, 97
Hammerton, Huntingdonshire 82
Harris Elsie Kathleen 58
Harwich, Essex 63
Heighton Messrs., Thrapston 61
Henin-sur-Cojeul, France 38
Hensman Alfred, builder, Thrapston 8
Hensman Mr., grocer, Thrapston 52
HIAM Robert Lewis 57, 97
HILL John William 85, 99
Hill Street, Kettering 12
Hill 60, Gallipoli 16
HODSON Alfred Ernest 82, 99
Holborn Workhouse, London 21
HOLLEY Percy John 21, 30, 98
Holley Mrs. Sarah Jane 21, 30
Hunstanton, Norfolk 38
Huntingdon 42

Ipswich Sanatorium 63
Iraq 93, 95
Ireland 7
Ironstone quarries and mines 13, 65
Isle of Man 90
Isle of Wight 7
Islip, Northamptonshire 10, 16, 50, 65
Islip Furnaces 4, 15, 29, 62, 77, 85

JACKSON Christopher 79, 99
Jackson Sir Thomas Graham, Bart., R.A. 104
JEFFERY Arthur William 45, 97
Jersey 23
JOHNSON Frederick William 73, 98, 124
JOHNSON George 49, 73, 97, 124
Jutland, Battle of 23

Kantara, Egypt 56
Kelly's Directory of Northamptonshire 115
Kettering, Northamptonshire 15, 26, 50, 53, 57, 58, 60, 84, 87
      Central School 78
      Grammar School 37
      Guardian 22, 37
      Hill Street 12
      Leader 28, 115
Kimbolton School 81
Kingsford Miss. 37
Kirby Lillian 55
Knight Denis 83. 121
Konigswartha Hospital, Germany 79
Kosovo 94

Langemark, Belgium 41
LANGLEY George Alfred 34, 98, 101
La Quinque Rue, France 9
Laxton Grammar School, Oundle 7, 80
Leeds, Yorkshire 78, 80
Leighton Bromswold, Huntingdonshire 83
LENTON Gerald 38, 98
Let not those kind F-words be lost 121
Loake Bros., shoemakers, Kettering 84
LOAKES Charles 66, 97, 124
Loakes W. & C., builders, Thrapston 66
Loaring & Son, outfitters, Thrapston 39, 79
LOARING William James 39, 97, 100, 110
LOVEDAY Alfred Shrives 50, 97, 101
Loveday Barbara 78
Lugg Harry, Driver R.A. 122

Macchiagodena, Italy 85
MAKIN Philip 3, 97, 114
Marconi International Marine Communication Co. Ltd. 7
Marlborough, Wiltshire 15
Marsh Ivy Mary 87
Marston, Bedfordshire 87

Marston St. Lawrence, Northamptonshire 31
Matania Fortunio 114
MAYES Ernest Harry 52, 97, 100, 103
Meadows Martha 4
Medals and Stars
    Defence Medal, WW2 111 113
    General Service Medal (Northern Ireland) 94
    Golden Jubilee Medal 2000 95
    Iraq Medal 95
    NATO (Kosovo) 94
    UN (Cyprus) 94
    Victory Medal, WW1 109
    War Medal, WW1 109
    War Medal, WW2 111, 113
    1914 Star 109
    1914/15 Star 109
    1939/45 Star 111
    Africa Star 111, 112
    Air Crew Europe Star 111, 112
    Atlantic Star 111
    Burma Star 111, 112
    France and Germany Star 111, 112
    Italy Star 111, 112
    Pacific Star 111, 112
Mehew Bill 13
Melbourne Road, Northampton 27
Mepal, Cambridgeshire 55
Mesopotamia 62
Midlands Cross Country Champion 15
Midland Railway 26
MILLER Herbert 33, 97, 124
MILLER Walter 3, 4, 33, 97, 114, 115, 124
Morehen Olive 43
MORLEY Joseph George 37, 97
Moulin-les-Metz, France 60
Mustachfa, Iraq 93

Naples, Italy 86
National Archive, Kew 53
NATO (North Atlantic Treaty Organisation) 94
Neuve Chapelle, France 8, 10, 31
NEWMAN Frederick William (Benny) 43, 61, 97, 100
NEWMAN Sidney 43, 61, 97, 100
New Town, Woodford 15
NICHOLLS George Ernest 28, 97, 115
Nicholls Mr., butcher, Thrapston 49
Niton, Isle of Wight 7
Northampton 4, 54, 61, 65, 72
Northampton Hospital 27
Northamptonshire Union Bank 64

Northern Ireland 93, 94
Norway 77, 117
Nottingham 31, 89
Nuneaton, Warwickshire 53

Old Weston, Huntingdonshire 89
Operation TELIC 95
Oundle, Northamptonshire 13, 80, 88, 90
Oundle School 80

Palestine 50
Paprat, Greece 27
Park Road, Raunds 55
Parker Kathleen 84
Partridge Mr., (Special Constable) 107
Peterborough 17, 88
Pettit Mr., builder, Thrapston 56
Pettit & Son, builder, Thrapston 104
Pilton, Northamptonshire 16
Pitts Olive 33
Pleasant Row, Islip 10
Ploegsteert, Belgium 44
Plymouth, Devon 77
Poland 79
POLLARD John Robert 14, 25, 97, 100, 101, 115, 116
Poperinghe, Belgium 4, 33, 55
Portland, Dorset 12
Primasole Bridge, Sicily 83, 119, 120, 121
Prince William School, Oundle 93
Prudential Assurance 87

Raby Mr., Postmaster, Thrapston 41
Ramsey, Huntingdonshire 58
Raunds, Northamptonshire 55, 86
RAWORTH Edward Percy 41, 42, 97, 100
REEVE Horace William 53, 97
REEVE William 9, 10, 97, 101
Regent Street, Northampton 54
Reningelst, Belgium 11
Rhodesia 80
RICHARDSON Charles Edward 16, 97
Riches Louisa 21
Roberts Rev. H.Ellis 43
Robinson Ada 22
ROGERS John 62, 97
Rouen, France 33
Rushden, Northamptonshire 32

Sacile, Italy 65
Sailly, France 13
Sainsbury J., Ltd 87
St. Andrew's School, Kettering 84
St.Ives, Huntingdonshire 55
St.Neots, Huntingdonshire 30, 53, 81
St.Paul's Cathedral, London 62
St.Paul's Churchyard, London, 41, 79
St.Quentin, France 59
St.Ruffine, France 60
Salerno, Italy 84
Salome Wood Farm Cottage 82
Salonika 21, 27
Sanderson Mrs. 107
Saskatchewan, Canada 24
Sennelager, Germany 93
SHADBOLT John Harry 71, 72, 97, 100
Shadbolt William, cycle dealer, Thrapston 71
Sharnbrook, Bedfordshire 62
Sharp Mr., (Special Constable) 107
Ships
    Acasta HMS 77, 117, 118
    Arankola SS 7
    Ardent HMS 77, 117, 118
    Ark Royal HMS 117
    Canada SS 7
    Dalhousie HMS 63
    Delphie HMS 7
    Ganges HMS 63
    Glorious HMS 77, 117, 118
    Gneisenau 77, 117
    Impregnable HMS 63
    LCT (Landing Craft Tank) 572 84
    Leviathan HMS 23
    Lord Gough SS 13
    Oriana SS 7
    Proserpine HMS 63
    Scharnhorst 77, 117, 118
    Tipperary HMS 23
    Westfalen SMS 23
Sicily 83, 84, 85, 119
Simeto River, Sicily 83
SIMPSON George Henry 17, 97
Smith Mrs. G. 108
SMITH George William Kenneth 64, 97, 100
SMITH John Samuel (Jack) 26, 97, 124
SMITH Robert Thomas 84, 99, 122
Soissons, France 53
Somme, France 25, 31, 34
Spalding, Lincolnshire 16
Spencer Street, Raunds 55

Sphere The 114
Stanion Mrs. Mary, Islip 21
STIMPSON John Thomas 58, 97, 124
Stothert Rev. B.W. (Rector of Thrapston) 104
Streaton, Illinois, USA 13
SUTCLIFFE John Isaac Ashton 24, 97
Swineshead, Bedfordshire 62

TANEY Alfred William 80, 99
TARRANT Arthur 56, 97
TEMPLEMAN Richard Edis 12, 14, 15, 25, 97, 116
Thompson & Sons, Peterborough 104
Thorpe Waterville, Northamptonshire 87
Thrapston
    Baptist Church 22, 30, 39, 41, 42, 43, 61, 63, 71, 98, 100
    Bell Ringers 62
    Bridge Street 38, 43, 52, 59, 63, 71
    Cemetery, Oundle Road 4, 26, 33, 49, 58, 63, 66, 73, 89
    Chancery Lane 24, 28, 40, 58
    Church Lane 28
    Church Villas, Chancery Lane 58
    Co operative Hall 107
    Corn Exchange 107
    Elm Farm 45
    Fair Lane 24
    Fire Brigade 9, 10, 65
    Football Clubs
        Argyll 14
        Crusaders 87
        Thursday 78
        United 13, 43, 65
    Grove Road 73
    Halford Street 3, 9, 13, 25, 26, 32, 50, 51, 52, 87, 90, 116
    Harriers Athletic Club 15, 78, 87
    Highfield Road 84
    High Street 54, 73, 88, 90
    Horton's Lane 31
    Huntingdon Road 14, 41, 42, 43, 45, 49, 61, 78, 82
    Journal (Thrapston, Raunds & Oundle) 83, 84, 106, 122
    King John Middle School 93
    King's Arms Hotel 43
    Manor House 40
    Market Road 21, 23, 29, 30, 41, 57, 62, 63, 72
    Men's Adult School 9
    Midland Road 11, 27, 58, 78, 86, 90
    Montague House 40
    Neneside 11
    Orchard House 64
    Oundle Road 3, 4, 10, 16, 17, 33, 59, 65, 83
    Parish Council 104, 106, 108

Peace Memorial Park 108
Poor Law Institution 108
Post Office 7, 41, 42
Primary School 93
Rifle Shooting Club (Thrapston & District) 103, 104
Ruston's Agricultural Engineers 93
St.James' Parish Church 3, 8 – 15, 26, 37, 39, 56, 62, 71, 72, 78, 97, 98, 99, 104, 108
    Church Choir 3, 13, 32, 50, 57
    Reredos 105
School 7, 21, 27, 31, 40, 51, 57, 63, 77, 78, 79, 82, 83, 86. 87
Scouts (1st Thrapston) 3, 4, 9, 10
Shop Assistant's Social Club 22
Shrubberies The 107
Smith & Grace 13, 25, 26, 34, 41, 50, 60, 64, 90, 93, 98, 101
South Terrace, Market Road 23, 27
Swan Hotel 37
Temperance Hall 106, 107
Titchmarsh Lane 4, 33, 59, 65
Town Band 9, 10, 57, 78, 107
Town Council Offices 101
Union 21
Victoria Terrace 8, 15
Washington Street 84, 85, 122
White Hart 38
White Hart Backway 57
THROSSELL Leonard 40, 98
Titchmarsh, Northamptonshire 12
Titchmarsh School 83
Touch A.H., outfitters, Thrapston 22
Towcester, Northamptonshire 10
Trones Wood, France 34
TURNER George William 32, 98
Twywell, Northamptonshire 67
Twywell Ironstone Pits 9

Ukhrul, Burma 87
UNGER George Abery 21, 98
UN (United Nations) 94

Vermelles, France 17
Verne Citadel, Portland 12
Villes-Bretonneaux, France 52

Wadenhoe, Northamptonshire 16
WAGSTAFF Herbert Brown 87, 99
Wainfleet, Lincolnshire 37
WAITE Albert John (Jack) 12, 13, 14, 15, 98
Waite Albert, fishmonger, Thrapston 8

WAITE Alfred Edward 8, 10, 11, 15, 98, 109, 110
Wakefield, Yorkshire 78
Walsall, Staffordshire 12
Walsrode, Germany 93
Warmington, Northamptonshire 33
WARREN Arthur Edward 23, 98
Watts Mr., grocer, Kettering 83
West Side Street, Great Addington 66
Whitney Mr., , Pilton 16
Wilton Horace 108
Wimille, France 64
Winchester, Hampshire 93
Winnipeg, Canada 40
Woburn, Bedfordshire 22
Woodford, Northamptonshire 56, 66, 82
WRIGHT Arthur William 67, 98
WRIGHT Samuel 59, 98, 115

Yelden, Bedfordshire 62
Yorkshire 78
Ypres, Belgium 3, 11, 38, 43

Zillebeke, Belgium 22, 38

Finis

The Thrapston Crest.